بِسْمِ اللهِ الرَّحْمٰنِ الرَّحِيمِ

THE DIGITAL PATH TO

VIRTUE

WHEN CLASSDOJO MEETS ISLAMIC VALUES IN THE CLASSROOM

MOHAMMED SALEEM, PhD

Universal Edu Enterprises Inc.
Ottawa, Canada

THE DIGITAL PATH TO VIRTUE: WHEN CLASSDOJO MEETS
ISLAMIC VALUES IN THE CLASSROOM

ISBN: 978-1-7775221-2-4

Published by:

Universal Edu Enterprises Inc. – Ottawa, Canada

Author: Mohammed Saleem, PhD
Cover Design: Fatima Saleem

DEDICATION

To my parents, may Allah ﷻ have mercy on them. They taught me the value of tradition in an age of innovations.

CONTENTS

PREFACE

All praise is for Allah ﷻ, Lord of all that exists. O Allah, send peace and blessings upon Prophet Muhammad ﷺ, the last of Your ﷻ messengers and prophets, and upon his ﷺ family, his companions, and all those who follow in his footsteps until the end of time.

My doctoral dissertation explored the use of computer technology in U.S. full-time Islamic schools. I was particularly interested in how technology was used by Muslims to teach and learn. A key theme I examined in my dissertation was the tension between tradition and innovation. Teachers and students in these Islamic schools continually negotiated the tension between the need to preserve the students' Islamic identity and their belief in the liberating potential of technology. In this book, I use ClassDojo, as the technology platform, to delve deeper into this theme.

Technology is rarely neutral. It is a double-edged sword that can enhance and amplify certain aspects of our life while backgrounding others. Often, there are unintended consequences with the use of technology. I chose ClassDojo because of its rapid adoption in schools across the world. Many Muslim educators have also adopted the technology in their classrooms without giving serious thought to its impact on the Muslim identity.

I have drawn on contemporary research that critically examines the use of ClassDojo to identify the issues and themes associated with its use in the classroom. Though most of that research comes from a secular and a materialistic lens, I have found that it still resonates with many Muslim concerns. To the best of my ability, I have questioned the underlying assumptions behind the conclusions in these studies and re-examined them through the worldview presented in the Qur'an and the *Sunnah*, as well as my personal experience using ClassDojo in an Islamic school. I have made a conscious effort to be as explicit as possible when doing so in the hopes that it will also motivate my readers to also think critically when using ClassDojo and other technologies.

I've offered many tools, tips and recommendations that I hope you will find useful in integrating technology in the classroom. I have used many Islamic terms in their original form in Arabic as it is difficult to find an equivalent in English. I have italicized those terms to let you know that their meanings can be found in the Glossary at the back of this book.

Islam and Muslims are at the forefront of global attention. Technology has been leveraged by Muslims for self-advocacy, but it has also been weaponized against Muslims, contributing to the rise in Islamophobia. Muslim educators must critically engage with technology to ensure its alignment with Islamic values. I hope the themes explored in this book inspire us to critically examine how we use technology and transform it and how, in turn, it transforms us.

May Allah ﷻ reward all who helped me in the preparation of this book. May Allah ﷻ accept this work and make it of benefit. First and last, all praise belongs to Allah ﷻ and may peace and blessings be upon our leader and teacher, Prophet Muhammad ﷺ.

Mohammed Saleem
2 Rajab, 1446 AH/2 January, 2025
Ottawa, Canada

1

DECONSTRUCTING THE CLASSDOJO BLACK BOX

M any of us use technology in our classrooms to fulfill various tasks as teachers and to deliver content without really thinking about how it is changing the way we teach and learn. Technology has revolutionized nearly every industry, and now this technological revolution has finally reached the largely unchanged education system.[1] The COVID-19 pandemic forced us to rapidly adopt technology in our classrooms as many schools switched to online schooling. Teachers retooled themselves to adjust to the new learning environments. Many of us scavenged for apps and devices that would facilitate our online teaching without really thinking about how it would impact us. Even though the pandemic is over, many of us continue to use these apps and devices in our classrooms. As we adjust to the new norm and as tech becomes more embedded in education, we need to think critically about the impact it is having on the way we teach and learn with it and in the process are transformed by it.

There is general agreement that technology is non-neutral and is shaped by political, social, and cultural elements.[2] It embodies specific interests and values and enacts scripts for how it should be used with ethical implications. For example, an ATM machine has certain "built-in" assumptions in its design: a user will always stand in front of it, be able to view the screen, and input data in a timely manner. However, this may not be the case with someone with a disability. Consequently, there are ethical considerations that arise in terms of its design and how it is used that are informed by user accessibility and ability. We must take the same criteria into consideration when we use technology in our classrooms.

The integration of technology in our classrooms is driven by certain socio-political, economic, and cultural agendas and has ethical and moral implications.[2] It can lead to unintended consequences, both positive and negative. Technology changes the way we interact with our world and consequently how we perceive it. It can enable us or disable us as individuals and as a community. It can change the way we relate with Allah﷾ and can have a significant impact on our Muslim identity.

Muslims have differing views on technology, yet we continue to embrace it out of necessity.[1] In some instances, Muslims have transformed or repurposed the technology to help fulfill their Islamic duties and observances and the technology contributed to the development of the Muslim identity. However, there have been many other instances where new technologies have eroded the Muslim way of life by proliferating a culture and values that are at odds with the Islamic way of living.

As educators, we do not have the luxury of experimenting with technologies in our classrooms without mitigating the potential harm from its use. We must ask how does the adoption of technology in our classrooms changes the way we teach and learn and what impact does it have on the development of children? What impact does it have on their identity?

I am going to use ClassDojo, a relatively new technology that has been rapidly adopted by teachers across the globe and even in Islamic schools, to explore issues related to the adoption of technology by Muslims. Like most technologies, the pace at which ClassDojo has been adopted has not allowed us to critically assess its impact on teaching and learning. It is important that we step back and closely examine the impact of such technologies. Though I use ClassDojo as the backdrop for analyzing the impact of technology, the themes highlighted in this book can be applied to assess the impact of other technologies on us. They provide a useful framework to live as a Muslim in the digital world.

What is ClassDojo?

ClassDojo is a behavior management app that allows teachers to award "dojo" points to students in real-time under default categories such as "hard work," "participating," "helping others," "teamwork," etc.[3] Teachers can add customized behavioral targets, which makes it possible to add culturally relevant and Islamic behaviors. Teachers can also give "warnings" or deduct points to students that result in a "ding" alerting the student and even the whole class that someone has received or lost a point.

Each student is represented by a cute monster avatar that can be customized by the student. Teachers can produce time series visualizations for each student to show their progress over time or display relative progress against the whole class as a leaderboard. Parents receive real time updates on their child's behavioral progress. Teachers, students, parents, and other stakeholders can track progress of student classroom/school behavior on their personal devices over a short as well as a long period of time making it easier for parents to follow up with at least part of their child's progress.

Schools can sign up for ClassDojo thereby enabling administrators to setup shared classrooms. Teachers and school leaders can "safely" share photos, videos, and messages with parents connected to the school in real time. This has greatly facilitated communication between the school and parents, replacing cumbersome flyers, newsletters, websites, and email groups.

A Popular App in Education

ClassDojo was launched in the August of 2011. Now it is actively used in more than 95% of US K-8 schools, more than 70% of Canadian elementary schools, and in more than 180 countries.[2, 4] Many of those countries are Muslim majority countries and I am anecdotally aware that several Islamic schools in US and Canada are also using it. Adoption of ClassDojo by teachers increased even more during the COVID-19 pandemic as many classrooms switched to virtual classrooms.[2] ClassDojo has recently expanded its offering in its "ClassDojo Beyond School" program where parents can manage their children's behaviour in home-based activities and "character building tasks".

ClassDojo won the Crunchie award for best education startup from the TechCrunch awards in 2015.[5] It was recognized as a finalist in the Fast Company's 2016 Innovation by Design Awards from among 1,700 submissions across 41 countries as the most innovated and disruptive design solutions to today's business problems. It was recognized for its two features, Class Story and School Story, that allow educators to connect instantaneously with parents and students.[6]

Videogame-like Features

ClassDojo's avatars, point system, leaderboards make it seem more like a videogame than a behavior management tool. It also enables teachers and students to "game" the system where students can exchange points for various class rewards. In this sense, ClassDojo quantifies classroom behavior, transforming it into a measurable and publicly visible metric. Some have criticized ClassDojo's gamified approach to classroom behavior and see it as reinforcement of gaming behavior and desires in children.[5] Others see it as part of the ludic surveillance of children where player data is collected to be used for other purposes.

One study found sound notifications for positive points motivated students to strive towards classroom behavior.[7] Social Cognitive Theory has been used to explain how the notification sounds engage students in a cognitive process wherein they start thinking about enacting similar behavior patterns so they can win more points. The same applies to negative points wherein students start blacklisting behaviors that will make them lose points. ClassDojo targets student behavior while overlooking the negative impact on student emotions due to point deductions and its consequent influence on student motivation to learning. Teachers may need to adjust for gender differences as in some cases, deduction of points has impacted female students more negatively than male students.[8]

The Theoretical Foundations of ClassDojo

ClassDojo at its very foundations is a behavior management tool informed by a long history of behaviorist psychology rather than the positive psychological concepts such as growth mindset and character development.[5] It seeks to observe and modify the actions of children through operant conditioning. It is part of a long line of "teaching machines" dating back as far as the 1920s where machines were designed to dispense candy to children for correct responses.[9]

However, reinforcement alone doesn't account for the change in student behavior for students adjusted their behavior based on what they saw modeled by their teachers and classmates. This occurred whenever students observed another student receiving a point, they subsequently imitated that behavior in the hopes of receiving the same point. Consequently, scholars concluded that the impact of ClassDojo can be better explained by Bandura's Social Learning Theory that views learning as a cognitive process that takes place in social contexts and occurs through observation and imitation.[10] In this case the environment also plays a central role on student learning where environmental factors affect student learning and students also influence the learning environment.

The founders of ClassDojo explicitly describe its purpose as promoting character development and have cited the works of the following scholars as inspiration behind the app:[5]

- Journalist Paul Tough, the author of two books on promoting grit and character in children.[11]
- Character development research conducted with the US network of KIPP charter school.[12] Their work is based on the work of Martin Seligman, author of texts on "authentic happiness" and "flourishing". It focuses on seven highly predictive character strengths needed to lead productive lives: zest, grit, optimism, self-control, gratitude, social intelligence, and curiosity. ClassDojo's default categories of positive behavior reflect this emphasis on character development, happiness, perseverance, and grit.
- James Heckman and his work on the power of building character early in life. He is a professor of economics at the University of Chicago where he directs the Economics Research Center. His website on the Heckman Equation focuses on the

economics of human development and the economic gains to be had by investing in early childhood development.[13]

- Angela Duckworth, a professor of psychology at the University of Pennsylvania, where she studies grit and self-control to predict academic and professional success. These two traits are perceived as dimensions of human character, social and emotional competency, and non-cognitive human capital.[14]

- Doug Lemov, founder of "Teach like a Champion" training program. His work focused on building accountability systems for charter schools and classroom management training techniques.[15]

- Lee Canter's work on assertive discipline that focuses on positive behavior management.[16]

- Carol Dweck's work on the growth mindset is probably the most influential in the later development of ClassDojo. She leads the Project for Education Research That Scales (PERTS) at Stanford University. Historically she has worked with Martin Seligman on learned helplessness and attribution theory and later extended this to the concept of growth mindset. ClassDojo announced a partnership with PERTS in 2016 and collaboratively produced a series of animated videos that explain the growth mindset idea for teachers and students.

- The concept of neuroplasticity, a recent reconceptualization in neuroscience of the brain as an adaptive organ that constantly adapts to the social environment informs the attempt in ClassDojo to shape students' thinking by shaping their behavior.[17] The concept of neuroplasticity also informs the rationale behind growth mindset and is a translation of ClassDojo's partnership with PERTS.

The works listed above bring a combination of psychological and economic interpretations of teaching and learning in the design of ClassDojo. Linking neuroscientific notions to classroom behavior is problematic because neuroscience's work on linking psychological theories to actual behavior is still in its infancy and tends to either confirm or negate existing theorizations of behaviors. Additionally, we need to be careful in applying the newly developed concepts of neuroplasticity to existing educational practice as many educational practices are based on a behavioristic framework.

ClassDojo combines behaviorist reward systems with behavioral surveillance to modify children's behavior via conditioning without considering one's thoughts or feelings.[10] This raises some important questions: Since ClassDojo focuses on observable behavior, how can teachers train students in the Islamic concepts of sincerity of intention and altruism? How can they guide students towards intrinsic motivation to meet expectations instead of students expecting rewards every time they meet their goals?

The theories that inform ClassDojo are secular and do not consider the spiritual dimension. In Islam, *shaytan* is an active influential element in human decision making. His goal is to divert us from the obedience of Allah❈ and push us towards the disobedience of Allah❈. He does this by whispering suggestions, deflating our energy, skewing our perspectives, etc. Muslim teachers and scholars from before paid great attention to this. Imam Al-Hafiz Abu'l Faraj ibn Al-Jawzi's monumental work *Talbis Iblis* (The Devil's Deception) is a great example of such a classical work where he discusses in detail the ways used by Shaytan in deceiving and leading humankind away from the Straight Path.[18] Teachers should become familiar with such literature and teach students how to protect themselves from *shaytan's* influence as part of their classroom management plan and strategy. So, for example, a strategy could be that we ask students who have not been paying attention in class or are tired and unable to focus, to go make wudu. This will not only refresh them physically but also perform a spiritual cleansing that will drive *shaytan* away and invite angels to be in their company.

Does ClassDojo promote student academic achievement?

In one study, eight out of ten teachers believed that there is a strong correlation between ClassDojo and students' academic performance.[10] Teachers have stated that it is effective in redirecting student behavior to meet classroom expectations and norms, which may inform student academic achievement.[8] Additionally, it was observed to increase the frequency of parents' involvement in their child's academic progress. However, experimental studies investigating such correlations do not exist yet. Moreover, the continuous evaluation of student behavior where everything is quantified removes students' focus from learning to behavior management.

Affordances of the ClassDojo Platform

Affordances are properties of a technology that relate to how it functions or can be used.[2] Affordances foreground certain ways of accomplishing a task while backgrounding others. For example, a staircase and a ladder can both be used for climbing. However, a staircase is perceived as facilitating the climbing of floors more than a ladder is because of certain affordances that the staircase provides. It does so while compromising on climbing speed since it uses an incline for more safety but in the process increases the distance between each floor. Likewise, a Kindle is used for reading books but cannot be used the way we use an iPad. Thus, affordances are defined by the material constraints and design of technologies. What affordances does ClassDojo have and how does it facilitate certain teacher tasks while backgrounding others? This is an important question for educators to answer as it will help us to identify and mitigate any gaps in student learning that may occur due to the use of ClassDojo in the classroom.

Class Story and School Story are two features of ClassDojo that allow administrators, teachers, students, and parents to communicate and share moments from the classroom.[5] They are instantly accessible on any mobile device or desktop via an updated stream of messages in the ClassDojo App. The messages can contain photos and videos. This feature provides a powerful yet simple "social media type" platform for teachers to share "protected" information of their students with the parents in a closed online community.

"Events" is another feature that allows educators to inform the school community in real-time of upcoming events. Automatic reminders can be setup to be sent out to parents as the event approaches. This has greatly facilitated schools in getting the word out to the school community about upcoming events.

ClassDojo also has a message feature that groups all communication between two users into a single thread. This makes it easier for teachers to keep track of communication between each of the several parents they usually interact with. This is better than email which usually ends up having several threads for each parent, making it difficult to keep track of all the communication.

ClassDojo provides a one stop platform for all the communication needs between the school and the home. Class Story, School Story, and Events are some of the features that have helped ClassDojo gain popularity among educators around the world without spending a dime on marketing.[19] However, it is the messaging feature that most users are using consistently and daily. All these communication features follow patterns of contemporary digitally connected communication that we see in social media.

Blurring work and personal boundaries

Technologies such as ClassDojo that greatly facilitate real-time communication tend to blur work and personal boundaries since parents can contact teachers at any time of the day or night. ClassDojo has a "quiet hours" feature where teachers can choose to turn it on if they do not want to be disturbed at specified times.[19] When turned on, parents receive an autoreply showing that the educator is currently unavailable. This feature allows educators to set the boundaries between work and personal time.

Translation feature makes communication more accessible

"Translate" is another feature of ClassDojo where messages are automatically translated into more than 35 different languages depending on whatever language parents have their phones set to.[19] How much has this facilitated home-school communication remains to be seen as there are other apps such as Google Translate that provide integrated translation across several apps on a mobile device.

Monitoring school communication

Educators can see which parents in the class have seen their post. This does not necessarily mean that they have "read" the post. Though this may fulfill educators' responsibility to communicate with parents, it doesn't necessarily mean that they have communicated with them. The platform also allows administrators to monitor communication on the platform between teachers and parents.

What's the verdict from the users?

Users have mixed opinions about ClassDojo. Many like it and advocate for it. Some are critical about it. Others are against using it in the classrooms and see it as an invasion of privacy. The majority, though, are silent users that use it just to go with the flow. This pattern of user reactions is common across technologies because the rapid pace at which technology is deployed and adopted doesn't allow room for the users to critically assess the technology. Let's look at what each major user of ClassDojo thinks about the app.

What do students think about ClassDojo?

Highschool students like ClassDojo.[8] Female students gave more favorable reviews of the app than male students. They felt that ClassDojo helped them to meet the expectations of their teachers and families. They also agreed more that the timely feedback from ClassDojo helped them see the behaviors they are good at. It is important to teach students how to use the feedback from ClassDojo productively. I wonder how many teachers take the time to do this or do we just stop short of score keeping?

What do teachers think about ClassDojo?

ClassDojo is popular among teachers as a monitoring tool where they can hold students accountable for their behavior, provide immediate and specific feedback, monitor their progress, and communicate with parents and other teachers.[20] A common sentiment amongst teachers is that it is easy to use ClassDojo. The platform greatly facilitates keeping track of student behavior and communicating with parents.[8] Its point-based system has generated vehement debate among teachers, principals, and parents with some considering the option to display students' scores equivalent to public shaming.[21]

Teacher interest in the platform increased considerably convinced by various studies that have highlighted the positive impact of ClassDojo on student motivation, engagement, discipline, cooperation, and attendance.[7, 22] Some have even attributed ClassDojo for promoting growth mindset traits in students.[23] However, a lot of the research on ClassDojo remains teacher centric and anecdotal, failing to use the experimental design to conclusively show its impact on student learning outcomes.[6]

What do parents think about ClassDojo?

In one study, parents of KG students did not feel that ClassDojo had a major impact on their child's behavior.[24] Parents stated that ClassDojo helped them to stay informed about their child's classroom behavior.[8] It also made it easier for them to communicate with the school. They attributed the app to helping them resolve some of the challenges their children were facing at school. Other parents despise it and consider it to be nothing more than a "cartoony bribe system" that is trying to manipulate student behavior to some predetermined norms and expectations.[21]

Parents wanted more clarity on ClassDojo's privacy policies as it was difficult to understand all the legalese.[10] Some felt the public display of points was equivalent to public shaming of students. While parents appreciated ClassDojo's facilitation of communication between home and school, they wanted teachers to use multiple strategies such as individual conversations, smiles, and verbal praise to redirect students and manage student behavior.

Varied implementation of ClassDojo

Teachers' implementation of ClassDojo in the classroom varies.[21] Some teachers display the app on their smartboards or classroom screens with the notification sounds turned on so everyone in the class can hear and see the awarding and deduction of points and know how many points each student has. Other teachers use it on "private" mode with the notification sounds turned off and only the teacher knows the students' points status. Some of these teachers also use other strategies such as talking with students privately to redirect them. Many teachers also leverage the secondary features of ClassDojo such as the random student picker, timer, and attendance and consider ClassDojo to be a primary classroom management tool.[10]

What impact do the different approaches to implementing ClassDojo have on student learning and their identity development? What do we gain and lose from each approach? Something that is quite common across all approaches is the lack of discretion that is being exercised by teachers when implementing such an invasive technology in the classroom. Most teachers are focused on the immediate gains, and few are reflecting on the long-term impact of using such behavior modification technologies on student development.

The intentional agenda and black boxing of ClassDojo

Often, we use a piece of technology without fully understanding how it functions. For example, we use a smartphone without really understanding the innerworkings of the device. Many of us do not understand the complexity of a smartphone with millions of transistors, sensors, and layers of software because it requires specialized knowledge and skills. We care only for its functionality without really appreciating what it takes to make such a complex device easy to use. When an internal workings, design, or operations of a technology get hidden or obscured from users then we say that it gets "black boxed".

Williamson has highlighted how ClassDojo has become a key black boxed technology of "government at a distance" to enable their social and emotional learning agenda.[4] This has been achieved through the process of translation; a process where human and non-human elements work on each other to translate or change each element until it becomes part of a stable network of actions and things to achieve specific goals.[2,] [25] Once a network is stabilized into a particular object, such as ClassDojo, it acts like a black box, immutable and concealing the negotiations that brought it into existence and disguising how each element has been transformed, distorted, and modified. This has been cited as a key technique of government exercised at arms-length through which they seek to achieve their goals and agendas from "a distance".[25] In this sense, the role of the government changes from that of a "protector" to one as an "investor" where children are reduced as a resource to be invested in for future socio-economic gains.

ClassDojo is a black boxed technology that has come into existence through a relatively stable network of psychological, governmental, and Silicon Valley discourses.[4] The ClassDojo platform allows each of these entities to work together while remaining distinct and independent. Government agencies, entrepreneurs, pressure groups, academics, managers, educators, and parents have come together to achieve a specific socio-emotional learning agenda by implementing it in schools.

ClassDojo brings together the Silicon Valley venture investment and venture labor with academics at Stanford University to employ new psychological and neuroscientific understandings. It has become a conduit for the growth mindset movement coming out of Stanford's

PERTS lab. It is also associated with the rise in government initiatives to measure children's social-emotional skills and behavior modification training programs. The US Department of Education's report on Promoting Grit, Tenacity and Perseverance highlights the same key messages from growth mindset and ClassDojo.[26]

Contested psychological and neuroscientific ideas about malleable mindsets and neuroplasticity have been encoded into the black box of ClassDojo and are being taken for granted. With its rapid adoption around the globe, it has become a powerful persuasive technology through which children are being measured, surveilled, valued, and made susceptible to behavior modification to achieve a specific socio-economic agenda that is very secular and materialistic in nature.[4]

Conclusion

The first words revealed to Prophet Muhammad ﷺ were:

$$ٱقْرَأْ بِٱسْمِ رَبِّكَ ٱلَّذِى خَلَقَ$$

Read: In the Name of your Lord who created. (Quran 96:1).

These words clearly identified learning and education as the main vehicle for the transformation and development of the Muslim *ummah*. The ClassDojo technology severely disrupts the way we teach and learn. Muslims, as marginalized and subjugated people that are susceptible to manipulation, must carefully evaluate the impact of a powerful persuasive technology such as ClassDojo before we adopt it in our classrooms. We must deconstruct the black box of ClassDojo to reveal its innerworkings so we can make informed decisions regarding its implementation in teaching and learning. This will help us to not only understand the intended goals and objectives of this technology but also to anticipate the unintended consequences of such a transformative technology.

2

CLASSDOJO AS DATAISM'S PROPHET AND MESSENGER

If someone wants to know what we wear, eat, listen to, etc., all they must do is search online. With the dominance of social media and related technologies, our data has become readily available online. While some see this as a serious problem regarding personal data and privacy, others view it as the beginning of a brighter and more liberated future. This belief in the liberating possibilities of technology has been termed by some as the technological sublime.[1] It is a "Saint-Simonian", utopian hopefulness that gives us a sense that technology can break the chains of our dreary, daily work routines and can lead to a world free of problems. This faith in technology, according to some, is giving rise to new religions and new ways of living.

ClassDojo is one of the expressions of the technological sublime. Its adoption by schools is spreading rapidly across the world. And its integration across various aspects of schooling is becoming more pervasive. This appropriation of ClassDojo is driven by the belief that such technologies can make the work of educators more efficient, effective, and easy. However, educators are not pausing long enough to reflect on the impact of such technologies on ways of schooling and eventually on ways of living. It is important that we unpack the bigger picture under which all of this is occurring as it will give us a deeper insight into the implications of using a technology such as ClassDojo in the important task of schooling of our children.

Emergence of Techno-Religions

Connected technology and Big Data, is leading to new religions and new ways of living. Some have called these religions techno-religions.[27] These techno-religions can be divided into two main categories: techno-humanism and data religion. Humans are supposed to distill data into information, information into knowledge, and knowledge into wisdom. However, some contend that we are unable to deal with the immense flow of data. Data religions view humans as inadequate to carry the torch of progress and instead need to hand it over to new entities such as AI. Techno-humanism still views humans as the apex of creation but seeks to enhance the physical and mental capabilities of humans with new technologies and genetic engineering to deal with the new reality of Big Data.

Although some argue that new technologies will create new gods and religious movements, rendering old religions obsolete or incapable of addressing contemporary challenges, I disagree with this view.[28] Religions have previously encountered disruptive technologies but were still able to adapt to the changes brought about by new technologies. The process of adaptation may sometimes change the way we practice our religion while at other times the technology might be modified to further enhance the traditional practices of the religion or both.[1]

However, old religions remain and continue to inform our ways of living.

Technology influences the way we view the world and how we operate within it. In that sense, it can lead to new religions for people who are not already anchored to an existing religion. Therefore, it is important for Muslims to approach the use of new technologies with a critical lens so we can mitigate any unintended negative consequences on the practice of our faith.

Dataism has been identified as one of the data religions.[28, 29, 30,] The worldview of dataists, the adherents of this religion, is informed by Internet based technologies and Big Data. They seek to reorganize the way we do things. ClassDojo is part of this paradigm. It is important for us to unpack this ideology as many Muslims are knowingly and unknowingly involved in this process of reorganization without realizing the potentially unintended consequences on Islam and Muslims.

What is Dataism?

First introduced in 2013, dataism has been described as a new form of religion that advocates the free flow of data as the greatest virtue towards salvation and prosperity.[28, 31] This is an extension of the technological sublime, the awe and belief in technology to save and liberate humanity.[1] Dataists, advocates of dataism, believe that the universe gives preference to those who contribute most to data processing. Since human beings were the most sophisticated data processing system, they were at the apex of existence. But big data and machine learning have surpassed human ability to process data; therefore, are more well positioned to be delegated the task of data processing and decision making.

Dataism may not look and feel like the traditional religions with their temples, churches, synagogues, and *masajid* and the rituals and lifestyles associated with those places. But a closer look will reveal that it has many of the elements of traditional religions. For those who believe in the technological sublime, Silicon Valley is the new Mecca for the religions of the 21st century rather than the Middle East.[27] Its temples are in the hallways of high-tech industry and the cyberworld. It may not be as distinguishable as the old religions in terms of its appearance, but its influence is far more pervasive as it occupies all aspects of contemporary living.

Dataism as a philosophy

Dataism is used to describe the philosophy influenced by Big Data. Brooks used it first to argue how this mindset based on Big Data can be used to reduce cognitive biases and illuminate patterns not revealed before to understand the increasing complexity of the world we live in.[31] Harari later described it as an emerging ideology and even a new form of religion where the flow of data is the supreme virtue to its adherents.[28] The artistic movement that centralizes data as a means of understanding the world has also been termed as dataism.[32]

Creating a utopia with technology

Like other faith-based groups, dataists believe in an Eden. This utopia is where everything is driven by the free flow of data. They envision a world where problems are solved before they become endemic. For example, AI can prevent epidemics from occurring through the continuous collection of biodata from all human beings that can detect any changes in the blood stream in a group of people in a region, identify the contagion, develop a vaccine, 3D print it, and deliver it to people's homes via drones, and direct them to take the vaccine. Likewise, continuous collection of children's educational data triangulated with data from other aspects of their life can guide AI to provide customized educational plans and interventions to minimize the achievement gap among all children. However, such utopian visions promising miraculous solutions fail to consider the Machiavellian tendencies of human nature and do not always unpack the threat of manipulation and exploitation that exists with access to Big Data.

Dataism is an existential threat to humanism

Some view the free flow of data and access to Big Data as an existential threat to humanism and to the idea of "free will". Dataism dismisses the core values of humanism and values raw data over human experience. It views humans as not only connected to other living things but also nonliving things in terms of their ability to process data. In such a worldview, the human being is not viewed as the apex of existence as there are other non-organic entities that can process data more effectively and efficiently than humans.

Dataism inverts the traditional system of learning. Traditionally, humans were the top processing unit that transformed data into information, information into knowledge, and knowledge into wisdom. However, dataists contend that humans are incapable of dealing with big data and this task should be instead delegated to external algorithms with greater data processing power. The role of human beings in this scenario is reduced from one of deciphering data to just inputting data. As we generate and analyze more and more data, our decisions will be based more on machine data rather than human experience and intuition.[33]

ClassDojo quantifies children's behavior into data that can be used by machines to identify patterns and trends. Is this sufficient for teachers and parents to guide children? We will see that the source of knowledge and its purpose is very different in Islam. This has very important pedagogical implications in the nurturing and development of children.

Knowledge and wisdom in Islam versus Dataism

The concept of knowledge and wisdom in Islam and dataism differs significantly in terms of origin, purpose, and approach:

Table 1: Concept of knowledge and wisdom in Islam and Dataism

	Islam	Dataism
Origin	Allah ﷻ is the source of all knowledge and knowledge is a gift from Allah ﷻ. Knowledge is granted by Allah through direct Divine revelation as well as Divine guidance through human intuition, reason, and experience.	Knowledge is empirical and objective, and is acquired from observable phenomena through data collection, analysis, and computational models. Dataism rejects any considerations of knowledge that may be subjective, spiritual, or moral.
Purpose	The purpose of knowledge is to free us from servitude to others to the servitude of Allah ﷻ. In addition to personal enrichment and worldly success, it is deeply linked to a higher moral purpose and to attaining salvation in the Hereafter by pleasing Allah ﷻ. Wisdom is not just experiential knowledge but also Divine guidance (the highest level of wisdom).	The purpose of knowledge is largely utilitarian, to maximize efficiency, solve problems, and optimize decision making based on data. The goal is to improve and enhance predictive accuracy. Knowledge is not just for individuals but also serves the global network where all systems are interconnected and optimized through the sharing of data. Wisdom is automated and achieved through algorithmic efficiency where machine-generated decisions are given primacy over human emotional intelligence, moral reasoning, and spiritual guidance.
Approach	Ethical considerations are deeply connected to Divine law, which provides the framework for discerning right from wrong, good from bad.	Ethical considerations are secondary and are meant to drive efficiency and optimization. There may be ethical guidelines for the use of data (privacy laws, etc.) but they are viewed as pragmatic concerns to ensure the smooth flow of data rather than as part of a larger moral framework.

It is important for Muslim educators to understand the philosophical differences between Islam and dataism as dataism becomes more entrenched with the proliferation of technology in our lives. This understanding will help us to equip our students with the critical lens they need to discern guidance from misguidance and good from bad as they try to live as Muslims.

This epistemological difference inextricably links learning to Divine guidance. For example, Allah ﷻ says in the Qur'an:

$$\text{...وَٱتَّقُوا۟ ٱللَّهَ ۖ وَيُعَلِّمُكُمُ ٱللَّهُ ۗ وَٱللَّهُ بِكُلِّ شَىْءٍ عَلِيمٌ}$$

And remain conscious of Allah, since it is Allah who teaches you. And Allah has full knowledge of everything. (Quran 2:282).

Allah ﷻ has linked *taqwa* to learning. The more we increase in *taqwa*, the more knowledge we will gain and the more knowledge we gain, the more our *taqwa* will increase.

The Prophet ﷺ has elaborated on how this reciprocal relationship between *taqwa* and knowledge works:

عَنْ أَبِي هُرَيْرَةَ رَضِيَ اللَّهُ عَنْهُ قَالَ: قَالَ رَسُولُ اللَّهِ صَلَّى اللَّهُ عَلَيْهِ وَسَلَّمَ :

"إِنَّ اللَّهَ عَزَّ وَجَلَّ قَالَ: مَنْ عَادَى لِي وَلِيًّا، فَقَدْ آذَنْتُهُ بِالْحَرْبِ، وَمَا تَقَرَّبَ إِلَيَّ عَبْدِي بِشَيْءٍ أَحَبَّ إِلَيَّ مِمَّا افْتَرَضْتُ عَلَيْهِ، وَمَا يَزَالُ عَبْدِي يَتَقَرَّبُ إِلَيَّ بِالنَّوَافِلِ حَتَّى أُحِبَّهُ، فَإِذَا أَحْبَبْتُهُ، كُنْتُ سَمْعَهُ الَّذِي يَسْمَعُ بِهِ، وَبَصَرَهُ الَّذِي يُبْصِرُ بِهِ، وَيَدَهُ الَّتِي يَبْطِشُ بِهَا، وَرِجْلَهُ الَّتِي يَمْشِي بِهَا، وَإِنْ سَأَلَنِي لَأُعْطِيَنَّهُ، وَلَئِنْ اسْتَعَاذَنِي لَأُعِيذَنَّهُ، وَمَا تَرَدَّدْتُ عَنْ شَيْءٍ أَنَا فَاعِلُهُ تَرَدُّدِي عَنْ نَفْسِ عَبْدِي الْمُؤْمِنِ، يَكْرَهُ الْمَوْتَ وَأَنَا أَكْرَهُ مَسَاءَتَهُ"

On the authority of Abu Hurairah ﷺ, who said that the Messenger of Allah ﷺ said: Allah ﷻ says: Whosoever shows enmity to someone devoted to Me, I shall be at war with him. My servant draws not near to Me with anything more loved by Me than the religious duties I have enjoined upon him, and My servant continues to draw near to Me with supererogatory works so that I shall love him. When I love him, I am his hearing with which he hears, his seeing with which he sees, his hand with which he strikes and his foot with which he walks. Were he to ask [something] of Me, I would surely give it to him, and were he to ask Me for refuge, I would surely grant him it. I do not hesitate about anything as much as I hesitate about [seizing] the soul of My faithful servant: he hates death, and I hate hurting him. It was related by al-Bukhari.[34]

This hadith illustrates how Allah ﷻ takes a central and very active role in our guidance and development. The more we connect with Allah ﷻ, the more we become knowledgeable about what pleases and displeases Him ﷻ. Therefore, Muslim educators must be focused on building their students' relationship with Allah ﷻ to achieve the goals of character development in Islam.

A reductionist philosophy

Dataism is a reductionist philosophy that reduces human beings into data. There are limitations to relying solely on data to understand human behavior and society. Like the gap between the android, Data, and his human companions in Star Trek, a human being is far more than just a data-processing entity. In Islam, the human being is the best expression of Allah's ﷻ creation and has been endowed with free will unlike the rest of the creation. Some have expressed concerns over the impact of datafication on free will and have asked if we will be the masters of the information or its slaves?

A data driven worldview

Dataism is a worldview that seeks to explain everything in terms of the flow and processing of data. For dataists, everything, from music to human behavior to emotion can be quantified into data. In such a world, the value of everything is based on their ability to process data. Everything can be explained in terms of data processing ability. For example, capitalism and the fall of communism can both be explained in terms of how they addressed the flow of data and the processing of data. Democracy can be viewed as a phenomenon of distributed processing of data while communism and dictatorships can be viewed as centralized processing of data.

Sometimes we see the approaches to solving the problems and challenges we face as Muslims are influenced by the worldview advocated by dataists. Leaders in our community sometimes tend to focus on the technicalities and the collection of more data and using that data to plan and organize. There is nothing wrong with this; however, it becomes problematic when we rely on that only and not give the same level of attention to how our decisions make others feel. Sometimes our goal becomes the efficient operation of our community institutions rather than the means through which we should be connecting people to Allah ﷻ.

Dataism promotes a secular worldview

Dataism is an expression of secularism. It is a worldview that trivializes Allah's ﷻ agency in the world by making technology the primary force. It understands the world in digitally informed ways. Dataists view the human species as nothing more than a single data processing system with individual humans as chips. Their goal is to connect us to more and more media to maximize dataflow. This would eventually lead to algorithms processing Big Data that humans would be unable to process. Consequently, we may delegate many important life decisions to these algorithms instead of to our religious and spiritual beliefs.

Dataism's emphasis on empirical evidence and scientific methods backgrounds the understanding of the world through faith or religious frameworks. It seeks to apply data-driven insights universally, promoting a sense of shared human experience and knowledge that transcends cultural and religious contexts. Its insistence on algorithms and data analysis diminishes the role of spiritual and religious interpretations of human existence and social phenomena. It views our experiences as part of a larger network of information thereby diminishing the importance of individual spiritual narratives and divine purpose. Its focus on continuous adaptability and change based on new information irrespective of any moral and ethical guidelines contrasts with the disciplined approach to life embedded in religious practices.

Dataism promotes a materialistic lifestyle

Dataism advocates a materialistic lifestyle that is driven by extensive analysis of observable data. It prioritizes material success with its focus on the quantification of various aspects of our lives, such as health, productivity, and social interactions. The data-driven insights used by businesses and marketers prioritize consumer preferences and behaviors, reinforcing a culture of consumptions where purchasing and acquiring goods are seen as pathways to happiness and fulfillment.

In such a lifestyle, maximizing productivity and efficiency via technology is intimately tied to the accumulation of material resources and wealth. Material possessions like gadgets and devices that facilitate data tracking and analysis are prioritized to promote a lifestyle focused on outward appearances and material benefits rather than holistic well-being. This makes us less engaged with non-material values such as attaining contentment through spiritual means as we see in the *du'a* of Prophet Muhammad ﷺ for contentment and blessings in whatever Allah ﷻ has provided for us.

Prophet's ﷺ *du'a* for contentment and blessings: Narrated by Ibn Abbas ﷺ that the Prophet ﷺ said:

أَللّٰهُمَّ قَنِّعْنِيْ بِمَا رَزَقْتَنِيْ وَ بَارِكْ لِيْ فِيْهِ وَاخْلُفْ عَلَىَّ كُلَّ غَائِبَةٍ لِّيْ بِخَيْرٍ

O Allah, make me content with what You have provided me, bless it for me and substitute every concealed (evil) with good (Al-Hakim 1/455).

Widens the power imbalance

Dataism focuses on overall trends and patterns and tends to ignore the details. But as the saying goes, "the devil is in the details". It is the details that provide the significance of an object, event, or phenomenon to the individual. If decisions are going to be made based on an understanding of trends and patterns, then those decisions may not always cater to the needs of individuals and specific groups. This becomes even more problematic when the direction of those trends and patterns is being intentionally dictated by those in power to promote their own interests.

Dataism promotes Islamophobia

Though dataism is not inherently linked to promote any form of prejudice, including Islamophobia, it can, in some cases, give rise to Islamophobia in indirect ways. Dataists believe that data is neutral. However, data is never neutral. Data-driven systems rely on historical data sets that may include biased representations of Muslims. When these data sets are used to train machine learning models or to make decisions related to immigration, law enforcement, and employment, they can perpetuate Islamophobic outcomes. In Chapter 3 I outline in more detail how surveillance and algorithmic profiling have contributed to power imbalances and to the rise of Islamophobia.

The Islamic worldview in a digitized world

Dataism focuses on how data can be used to validate (or invalidate) our deeply held assumptions about the world we live in. Therefore, it is important for Muslims to critically examine its impact on our lives as it directly impacts the way we view the world and live within it.

Table 2: Islamic worldview vs. the worldview advocated by dataism

	Life Elements	Dataism	Islam
1	Understanding of Reality	Reality is often reduced to data and algorithms, emphasizing measurable and quantifiable aspects.	Reality is multifaceted, encompassing spiritual, moral, and material dimensions.
2	Nature of Existence	Emphasis on interconnectedness of data and systems, often views existence through a scientific lens (only "observable" phenomena are considered valid).	Emphasis on interconnectedness of all creation. Everything exists within the framework of Allah's will and purpose. Our existence in this life determines the outcome in our life after death (the Hereafter).
3	The human being	Nothing more than a single data processing system with individual humans as chips.	Created by Allah with free will and with many faculties that allow the human being to make informed decisions for which we will be held accountable by Allah. *Tarbiyah* is needed to develop a sound heart that can discern right from wrong.[i], [35]

---

[i] Allah has given every human being the ability to discern right from wrong. Allah ﷺ says:

وَنَفْسٍ وَمَا سَوَّىٰهَا (٧) فَأَلْهَمَهَا فُجُورَهَا وَتَقْوَىٰهَا (٨)

And the soul and He who proportioned it. And inspired it with its wickedness and its righteousness. (Quran 91:7-8).

	Life Elements	Dataism	Islam
4	Human Purpose	To optimize decision-making and improve efficiency using data and algorithms. This seems to be the ultimate raison d'être.	To worship Allah, follow His guidance, and fulfill moral and ethical responsibilities. Optimized decision making and efficiency are part of the concept of *Ihsan* (excellence) to achieve this goal.
5	View of the Individual	Individuals are often seen as data points within larger systems, with less emphasis on individual agency.	Individuals have a unique purpose and are accountable to Allah for their actions. They have a role as *khalifa*.
6	Understanding of Community	Advocates for connectivity through data sharing, often prioritizing efficiency over personal relationships.	Emphasizes communal bonds, social justice, and collective responsibility.
7	Source of Knowledge	Data as the primary source of knowledge, emphasizes empirical evidence.	Allah is the source of all knowledge. Divine revelation (Qur'an, Hadith) guides experiential knowledge.
8	Moral Framework	Largely based on outcomes derived from	Grounded in the Quran and Sunnah.

We are expected to exercise this ability to make decisions in life. This ability is guided by the Quran and the Sunnah as explained in a farewell conversation between the Prophet 🕮 and Muadh ibn Jabal 🕮 as he was departing to Yemen:

حَدَّثَنَا حَفْصُ بْنُ عُمَرَ ، عَنْ شُعْبَةَ ، عَنْ أَبِي عَوْنٍ ، عَنِ الْحَارِثِ بْنِ عَمْرِو بْنِ أَخِي الْمُغِيرَةِ بْنِ شُعْبَةَ ، عَنْ أُنَاسٍ ، مِنْ أَهْلِ حِمْصَ مِنْ أَصْحَابِ مُعَاذِ بْنِ جَبَلٍ أَنَّ رَسُولَ اللَّهِ صلى الله عليه وسلم لَمَّا أَرَادَ أَنْ يَبْعَثَ مُعَاذًا إِلَى الْيَمَنِ قَالَ " كَيْفَ تَقْضِي إِذَا عَرَضَ لَكَ قَضَاءٌ " . قَالَ أَقْضِي بِكِتَابِ اللَّهِ . قَالَ " فَإِنْ لَمْ تَجِدْ فِي كِتَابِ اللَّهِ " . قَالَ فَبِسُنَّةِ رَسُولِ اللَّهِ صلى الله عليه وسلم . قَالَ " فَإِنْ لَمْ تَجِدْ فِي سُنَّةِ رَسُولِ اللَّهِ صلى الله عليه وسلم وَلاَ فِي كِتَابِ اللَّهِ " . قَالَ أَجْتَهِدُ رَأْيِي وَلاَ أَلُو . فَضَرَبَ رَسُولُ اللَّهِ صلى الله عليه وسلم صَدْرَهُ وَقَالَ " الْحَمْدُ لِلَّهِ الَّذِي وَفَّقَ رَسُولَ رَسُولِ اللَّهِ لِمَا يُرْضِي رَسُولَ اللَّهِ " .

When the Messenger of Allah 🕮 intended to send Mu'adh ibn Jabal to Yemen, he asked: How will you judge when the occasion of deciding a case arises? He replied: I shall judge in accordance with Allah's Book. He asked: (What will you do) if you do not find any guidance in Allah's Book? He replied: (I shall act) in accordance with the Sunnah of the Messenger of Allah 🕮. He asked: (What will you do) if you do not find any guidance in the Sunnah of the Messenger of Allah 🕮 and in Allah's Book? He replied: I shall do my best to form an opinion, and I shall spare no effort. The Messenger of Allah 🕮 then patted him on the chest and said: Praise be to Allah Who has helped the messenger of the Messenger of Allah to find something which pleases the Messenger of Allah 🕮.

	Life Elements	Dataism	Islam
		data analysis, which may lack a fixed moral framework.	
9	Ethical Considerations	Ethical considerations often arise in the context of privacy and data use but may lack a cohesive moral framework.	Strong emphasis on ethics, justice, and compassion as guided by the Qur'an and Sunnah.
10	Human Progress	The more data we generate and process and make most out of it the better and more liberated our lives will be.	Is measured by how many people we can free from the worship of creation to the worship of Allah ﷻ.
11	Approach to Change	Change is embraced, driven by data insights and the need for adaptability in a fast-paced world.	Change is viewed as part of divine wisdom; actions must align with ethical guidelines.
12	Role of Technology	Belief in the technological sublime. Technology is central, focusing on data collection and analysis to enhance understanding and efficiency. ClassDojo is a tool for datafication and analysis of children's behavior to gain deeper insight about children and to plan better aligned learning programs.	Tools and technology are means to worship Allah by serving humanity and thereby fulfilling divine purpose. ClassDojo can provide one of many data points to better understand children and their learning.

The table above provides a broad overview of the Islamic worldview and the worldview espoused by dataism. Each perspective offers unique insights into understanding existence, purpose, and ethics. Muslim educators must become intimately familiar with these differences as it will help us to guide our students in discerning right from wrong and guidance from misguidance. Understanding of the Islamic worldview and how it differs from other worldviews is central to becoming a critical consumer of technology.

Benefits of datafication

Dataists want to ensure the free flow of data. For example, if we were to allow our medical data to be used without restrictions then it would greatly facilitate medical researchers to find people with specific conditions for their research; thereby greatly accelerating the research process. The greater the access to people's data, the easier it is to spot patterns and gain insight into our world.

There are many advantages to the open use of data. Businesses can offer us customized products and experiences. Schools can use it to create customized learning plans for students. Research institutions can not only speed up their research but gain insights from Big Data that they would otherwise be unable to. Medical facilities can use data to save lives. However, if we are not careful about how we adopt technology, all of this occurs at a cost where we may be unknowingly sacrificing the infinite pleasures of the hereafter for the pleasures of this relatively short-lived life.

Conclusion

Dataism has also found its believers among Muslims who are not immune to the effects of the technological sublime. Some Muslims advocate leveraging Big Data to further strengthen the implementation of Islamic principles and laws for the greater benefit of the *ummah* (the global community of Muslims). For example:

1. *Zakah* can be more efficiently distributed by having AI triangulate multiple data points in real time to identify the most deserving.

2. *Shari'ah* compliant financial products can be better aligned to the Islamic law and made more accessible to Muslims by analyzing user data, financial trends, and data from a hoard of other variables that would be impossible for one sheikh or mufti to do.

3. *Hajj* can be optimized for everyone by analyzing crowd movements, facility usage data, weather patterns, etc.

4. *Halal* consumption can be made more transparent and better aligned with the Islamic principles by analyzing data from supply chains, product origins, manufacturing processes, environmental and eating patterns.

The possibilities of how Big Data can optimize the practice of the Islamic faith by Muslims seem to be endless and some see it crucial for Muslims to embrace this transformative power of Big Data to pave the way for a more enlightened and prosperous future for Muslims.

However, as we have explored in this chapter, dataism at its core is a secular philosophy that is at odds with the Islamic worldview at many levels. Additionally, it further marginalizes the Muslims. ClassDojo is one of the expressions of dataism and if we want to integrate it into our classrooms then we must do so carefully. The challenge for Muslims is to leverage this technology and other technologies in a balanced manner without compromising on the Islamic values and morals while mitigating the intended and unintended consequences of using that technology.

3

ISLAMIC PERSPECTIVES ON ETHICAL ISSUES IN CLASSDOJO'S USE OF CHILDREN'S DATA

People are unwittingly or naively entrusting their personal information to corporate platforms in exchange for services. This trust is rooted in the belief borne out of datafication where people trust their personal information to large corporations, government, and public institutions.[36] There is a widespread belief in the objective quantification and tracking of human behavior and social life through online media technologies. Dataists believe that free flow of data will lead to more freedom and prosperity. However, all these organizations are intimately interconnected within the same ecosystem, making it very difficult to maintain the objectivity of the data collected and to ensure it won't be exploited.

Datafication is increasingly being considered as the gold standard of knowledge about human behavior and is becoming the new social-scientific paradigm for entrepreneurs, academics, and government agencies. There are two basic assumptions behind this: 1. Data collected is objective, 2. *Metadata* is "raw material" that can be accurately and objectively analyzed to produce algorithms to predict future human behavior.

Datafication of our life

We are generating an unprecedented amount of data as our lives become more and more digitized. The amount of data generated by the *Internet of Things (IoT)* is astronomical and humanly unmanageable. This datafication of our lives has become a new paradigm as Big Brother and Big Business routinely access our personal information, aka Big Data. Mayer-Schoenberger and Cukier define datafication as the process of converting social actions into quantifiable online data, enabling real-time monitoring and predictive analysis.[37]

The use and tracking of data have many immediately obvious benefits. Google Maps successfully uses big data to help us navigate through congested traffic and even warns us of any police traps. Google has been able to predict illness outbreaks long before medical institutions by identifying online searching patterns (people searching more frequently for a certain symptom associated with an illness). Datafication is emerging as a valid approach to access, comprehend, and monitor human behavior, gaining traction not only among technology enthusiasts but also among scholars who view it as a transformative research opportunity to explore human actions.

Use of Data during the Prophet's ﷺ time

It is from the sunnah of the Prophet ﷺ that he would make informed decisions based on the data that he collected. Abu Bakr ﷺ continued this tradition and enhanced it further by having a network of messengers that not only kept him well informed but also kept him connected with his generals and administrators across the Arabian Peninsula. So, the collection of data for informed decision making to keep us safe and to enhance our lives is not against Islamic principles. The issue is the sincerity in determining the criteria used to collect data, the type of data that is being collected, and the purpose behind the collection of data.

An unintended consequence of datafication

One of the unintended consequences of datafication is that algorithms are designed to foreground data that is more popular thereby muting other data. Companies do this intentionally to boost their profits. Politicians and advocacy groups do this as well to promote their agendas. This free flow of data is hardly "free". It is directional and the directions are often dictated by those in power. This further exacerbates the gap between the majority culture and the minority cultures. Thus, Muslims remain an ambiguous, blurred, and muted group despite the so called "free" flow of data.

Uncritical acceptance of commercially driven datafication undermines the integrity of schools as sanctuaries of learning for our most vulnerable population, our children. Educators have a moral obligation to protect our children's education from being turned into a product to be used for commercial purposes. Hence, ClassDojo should be used carefully after making sure proper procedures are in place to safeguard privacy, security, and to prevent the misuse of data collected.

In 2017, *The Economist* proclaimed that data was the world's most valuable resource, surpassing even oil in worth.[38] Data is important for us to gain self-insight, improve and prosper as individuals as well as communities. Data holds unprecedented significance in shaping the future of society, culture, and even spirituality. Datafication and dataveillance are increasingly viewed as normalized practices as dataism, as a philosophy, becomes more and more accepted by the public. They are quickly becoming the online pillars of democracy and sociality.

Objectivity of Data

Data is never objective; rather, it is always derived through personal interpretations. There is a notion among dataists that skewed data can be ameliorated by studying patterns in large sets of data. However, there is a very high possibility that large sets of data can further magnify the initial skewedness present in the individual data sets.

The concept of "raw data" is an oxymoron. The quality of data collected can vary and it can be good or bad, incomplete and insufficient. The contexts; commercial platforms or public institutions, in which data is generated and processed can vary and shape the data. Yet we are using data interchangeably without giving due consideration to the sources used in generating that data.

Data by itself is not a raw resource waiting to reveal some unfound treasures. What we can learn from large quantities of data is dependent on the analytical methods we use to unpack it and the frameworks we use to interpret. Google may claim that it can forecast unemployment statistics or flu epidemics based on what people are searching for. Facebook claims to predict which young mothers are likely to not care for their children based on number of likes. And the NSA (National Security Agency) declares to have prevented so many terrorist attacks through the PRISM scheme. However, majority are unaware of the algorithmic criteria used to define what counts as job seeking, dysfunctional motherhood, and terrorism.[36] How such criteria are defined is driven by the worldview of those in power and by socio-political contexts. Such a process seeks to maintain and strengthen the existing unequal power structures and furthers the exploitation of the oppressed. Muslims, as an oppressed people, remain at the center of this target.

Data is value laden

Dataism and digitally driven convictions flourish on the assumption that data happens independent of any preset framework. However, data is always value laden and occurs in contexts that are driven by many factors and for specific purposes.[36] Those who leverage technologies, and mine and interpret data generated from its use do not always communicate explicitly the intent behind their efforts. A medical doctor, an engineer, and a school principal may look at the same data and come up with entirely different interpretations. As Big Data becomes more and more readily available, there is a need for transparency from tech companies. information scientists, and government agencies in terms of the criteria used to collect data, how the data is being used and to what purposes. Therefore, users must always approach the use of technology and any related data and its interpretations with a critical mindset.

Those endorsing the datafication paradigm consider social media data as "natural traces" and the respective platforms as "neutral" facilitators.[36] Big data collected from such platforms is viewed as more representative, comprehensive, and reliable than sampling, interviewing, or polling. They argue that the large size of the data compensates for the "messiness" of Big Data in contrast to the small amounts of sampled data. For example, Twitter has been called a sensor of real time events and even a "sentiment detector". However, Twitter users do not necessarily represent the demographics of the public. Only 15 percent of online adults use Twitter and only 8 percent use it daily.[36] Additionally, Twitter's algorithms favor influential users and allow for manipulation of tweet messages by the platform itself or by coordinated group of users. Despite its skewed representation of people's sentiments, the Twitter Political Index is being used as a legitimate way to measure public opinion and the media indiscriminately uses popular Tweets to shape public opinion and to legitimize dominant narratives.[39]

Weaponization of social media

Social media and other Internet technologies have been weaponized against Islam and Muslims with the rise in Islamophobia. Interconnected mechanisms such as data collection practices, algorithmic biases, and media influence have increased Big Data's potential to promote Islamophobia and reinforce harmful stereotypes and biases against Muslims. We need to prepare our children to thrive despite the challenges they will face as they grow up in a digitized world that may be hostile to their Muslim identity.

Data ownership

Another issue with the rise in datafication is who owns the data? Is it owned by the person to whom it relates to or the companies that collect it? Can those companies one day charge us to access our own data? Can they sell it to other companies without our permission?

ClassDojo collects immense amounts of data on children who are not really able to provide informed consent. Parental consent is required; however, parents do not have the time and in many cases the language proficiency and technical/legal knowledge to grant a truly informed consent for their child's information and data to be collected and stored.

It is difficult to anticipate how the collected data will be used. Companies routinely share user data with third parties and can even sell the data in the future. Given the unpredictability, opaqueness, and the many variables surrounding data ownership, the question we must ask is do we have the right to allow our children's data to be collected?

Loss of privacy

One of the biggest challenges to the datafication of our lives is the fear of loss of privacy. People are understandably concerned that data can be used to exploit and manipulate people. Businesses routinely do this to increase product sales. Governments have used Big Data to promote their programs. Politicians have used it to influence voters.

The Facebook-Analytica data scandal showed how political leaders manipulated Facebook's user data to manipulate the network. It involved the unauthorized collection of personal data from millions of Facebook users by the consulting firm Cambridge Analytica. Detailed psychological profiles were built from the data for targeted political advertising to influence the 2016 US presidential election and the Brexit referendum. The scandal highlighted issues with privacy, the ethical use of user data, and the lack of regulation surrounding data protection.

There has been a change in culture over time that has impacted the level of trust people put in sharing their personal data.[37] A few years back it was not normal for people to announce what restaurant they were eating at, the food they ate, and with whom they went to eat it. But now people are sharing much more than that on social media. This has largely occurred because access to necessary services and entertainment is granted by tech companies through an exchange of access to personal data.

Normalization of data sharing

We are more and more willing to give up our data in exchange for "freedom" and a better standard of living.[38] ClassDojo targets this same trend in culture change albeit at a very young age. Children are being normalized from a very young age to share their very personal data. As data becomes more deeply integrated into society, ethical issues related to data ownership, privacy, and consent are becoming increasingly important. Global regulation is essential, with frameworks like GDPR (General Data Protection Regulation) and CCPA (California Consumer Privacy Act) to guide the collection, storage, and use of data.[33] Like the GDPR and CCPA frameworks, Muslims must develop their own security and privacy framework based on the Islamic worldview.

The use of Big Data in education poses important ethical challenges regarding the protection and privacy of children because cybersecurity is still far from complete in this area. The potential for exploitation of data collected from these vulnerable populations can exacerbate existing inequities and introduce new inequities in the field of education. This is specially the case for Muslim children in an era where Islamophobia is on the rise.

Datafication of student behavior via ClassDojo

ClassDojo quantifies students' behavior and social interactions. It is part of the new paradigm of datafication where many aspects of our social life have been coded and quantified – friendships, interests, tastes, emotions, conversations, searches, etc. ClassDojo follows the same pattern of datafication with our children's behavior and social interactions in one of the most sanctified safe spaces in our society, the classroom.

Data is not always used in a sincere manner. For example, a weekly email update for school leaders begins with "Wow! Look how your school community came together last week" and then it lists numbers: 1,009 messages sent home, 54 stories shared, 2,354 skills celebrated, and 84% positive feedback.[19] The message then ends with "Now that's worth celebrating! Go on, share the good news" and has a confetti emoji at the end of the sentence. The data in the above example is used to promote further use of the ClassDojo app via generalized interpretations that may be skewed. This level of datafication that may be based on frivolous data can give a false sense of accomplishment and blur the reality on the ground.

Datafication of student behaviors and interactions in ClassDojo are providing new forms of interpretative value. Some warn that its uncritical adoption is facilitating real-time monitoring of students, leading to an imbalance of power, agency, and decision-making for both students and parents.[2] While students become visible and quantifiable, the power dynamics remain hidden, leaving learners focused solely on the task and their results. In this way, students are rendered manageable according to pre-specified criteria. What kind of critical attitude should we have when we are allowing our interactions at the school and our children to be subjected to the datafication of their behaviors and social interactions in the classroom and the school?

ClassDojo claims that the data it collects is encrypted and secure; however, many ethical and privacy concerns from parents and teachers remain unresolved.[2] It is difficult for many parents to understand the legal language on privacy policies on the company's website.[17] Additionally, its capacity to store data indefinitely not only raises privacy concerns but also concerns about how the data will be used and misused in the future.

What type of data does ClassDojo collect?

ClassDojo has an interactive *Information Transparency* policy page that specifies the types of data collected from various user groups, students, parents, and teachers. The data includes personal information, location details, and behavioral data but excludes health information. Personally identifiable information is collected but it is unclear whether biometric data is collected as well. Most of the data is automatically collected and it is not clear if opt-in consent is requested from users at the time personal information is collected.

ClassDojo also collects various types of data, including student behavior reports, classroom activities, and communication records. ClassDojo claims that personal information collected from students is never used for behavior targeted advertising.[40] However, this data is not only used to facilitate communication, track student progress, and support classroom management but also to inform educational policy and to improve the platform. For example, ClassDojo's feature of generating student summary reports of the points collected has been touted as useful in effective decision making by educators.[17] Do parents understand the implications of their children's data being collected and how it will be used?

The policy states that personal information is shared with a limited number of third-party providers to deliver and enhance services. The third parties and their roles are indicated, and third-party login is supported. These third-party providers are contractually obligated to comply with ClassDojo's privacy and security requirements.

The policy states that if ClassDojo finds that it has collected information from a child in violation of COPPA (Children's Online Privacy Protection Act), it will take the necessary actions to either delete the information or promptly obtain parental consent for the collection. Many privacy policies are difficult to read because of their length and/or use of technical/legal jargon that requires advanced reading skills. Parents simply may not have the time to read through most of these policies and to keep pace with the continuous changes they undergo. Therefore, the policies do not really have an educative component clearly indicating how parents can protect their children's data in ClassDojo. This is left for the parents to figure out.

Is it OK to collect data of young children?

Is it OK to collect data of young children where they may not have a say in that decision? One of the key guiding principles of the *Convention on the Rights of Children* ratified by Canada in 1991 is that all actions concerning children should be guided by the principle of the best interests of the child.[41] ClassDojo's policy states that if they collect children's information in a manner inconsistent with COPPA then they will either delete it or immediately seek parental consent.[40] However, Commonsense Media lists several privacy warnings for ClassDojo.

Warning rating from Commonsense Media

Commonsense Media gave a "Warning" rating to ClassDojo for the following:[40]

- Sharing personal information for third-party marketing.
- Displaying personalized advertising on the platform.
- Collection of data by third parties for their own purposes.
- User's information is used to track and target advertisements on third-party websites or services.
- Creates data profiles for personalized advertisements.

- User information is not de-identified when shared with third parties.

ClassDojo does indicate the categories of information shared with third parties, the purpose for sharing, the categories of third parties, and the contractual limits placed on third-party data use. All of this requires extensive reading and the ability to understand the technical jargon that is used in privacy policies, which may be difficult for most parents.

Is the data in ClassDojo safe?

ClassDojo holds the iKeepSafe FERPA Certification (Family Educational Rights and Privacy Acts), indicating that its website, platform, and apps have been reviewed and approved for compliance with federal FERPA regulations.[40] It does not allow students to post content outside of their classroom groups and no ClassDojo content is made available to the public. However, it remains to be determined if this enough to keep the data safe.

Data Deletion and Retention in ClassDojo

Responding to concerns about data collection of children raised by parents and educators, Sam Chaudhary, the co-founder of ClassDojo, said that they were not a data company and intend to delete the data after one year.[21] ClassDojo has a detailed data deletion and retention policy in order to comply with student privacy laws and maintenance of educational records such as the US Family Educational Rights and Privacy Act.[42]

Users retain ownership of their data and maintain it; however, this is disputable. Users with registered accounts can update, correct, or delete some of the user profile information or preferences at any time by logging into their accounts. However, they are not able to delete all the user data even if they close their ClassDojo account. If parents close their accounts, then all the history between the parent and the teacher in the classroom is automatically hidden (but not deleted) by ClassDojo.

I am aware of one incident where a parent was aware of this feature, and they intentionally left the classroom to "delete" some inappropriate messages they had sent to a teacher. The teacher was unable to view the communication record to document the abuse they had experienced from this parent. The school principal had to request ClassDojo to release the communication records for the teacher to be able view the messages. This extra step prompted the school principal to direct teachers to move all "official" communication that needs to be documented to emails.

Is the data truly safe on a mobile device?

Providing a secure platform is only one of the elements in securing user data. There are other gaps that need to be secured to protect user data. For example, it is difficult to monitor and guarantee that only the authorized users will use the device with which they are accessing ClassDojo. What happens if the device is lost, stolen, or lent to someone for temporary use? ClassDojo's user data is saved on teachers' mobile devices, which can jeopardize the security of the data. Is the teachers' digital literacy at a level that enables them to protect all data on their devices? Are there any precautionary measures they can take to protect their students' data during any unanticipated breaches of privacy and security?

Neutrality of the data collected in ClassDojo

Putting aside ClassDojo's contested claims that it is not a data mining company, we need to ask, can they maintain the neutrality of the collected data? Is that even possible? Those who claim this assume that online social traffic flows through neutral technological channels. However, that is not the case. Technology and the business models deploying that technology are never neutral.

One study, investigating ClassDojo as a facilitator of psychological surveillance through gamification techniques, examined the correlation between ClassDojo's psychological concepts and the physiological methods of Silicon Valley designers and concluded that ClassDojo was being used in schools to prioritize governmental interests to achieve political goals.[4] We have no guarantees from ClassDojo on the future uses of our children's data. Snowden's leaks exposed social media companies' sharing of user data with intelligence agencies.[29]

Government leaders have defended their practice of closely working with tech companies for data mining. Barack Obama, defending his administration's policies of mass surveillance, said that citizens cannot expect a hundred percent security and a hundred percent privacy without any inconvenience. Information and Privacy Commissioner of Ontario, Brian Beamish, while acknowledging the privacy concerns around ClassDojo said that the use of ClassDojo "should be setting off alarm bells" and that if he were a parent, he would have his eyes wide open.[41]

Inherent biases in ClassDojo

Many of the behavioral norms targeted in ClassDojo are derived from contested psychological categories.[5] These targeted norms are achieved through behavioral surveillance and reinforced through behaviorist reward systems. Though ClassDojo's founders insist that the focus is on positive behavior reinforcement, the targeted behaviors may or may not align with values of minority cultures and with Islamic values. Teachers should carefully review the targeted behaviors to make sure that the powerful reinforcement provided by ClassDojo inculcates social and emotional attributes and attitudes that are aligned with the desirable character of the ideal Muslim.

Some important questions we must ask: Since ClassDojo focuses on observable behavior and extrinsic motivation, how can teachers train students in the Islamic concepts of sincerity of intention and altruism? Since ClassDojo allows government and educators to leverage social norms derived from a specific culture (a secularist culture) at a scale and in a manner unprecedented, what impact does this have on minority cultures, specially of those faith-based minorities that are viewed negatively?

Globalized surveillance and part of the neo-colonial apparatus

Classrooms are supposed to be safe environments where our children can gain knowledge and learn important life skills and become contributing members of the societies that we live in. Countries that have privacy laws provide some level of protection to their citizens from invasive technological practices such as those observed in the implementation of ClassDojo. However, as the app becomes widely adopted around the globe and in countries where privacy laws may not be as robust or consistently implemented or government may not have a system of checks and balances, we must give serious consideration regarding the harvesting of children's information and its potential misuse in the international global market and the global security apparatus.

Many Muslim majority countries do not have robust privacy laws and/or may have laws and apparatus designed to maintain the continued economic, political, and cultural influence of their former colonizers.

Many are operating under a crisis and are ill equipped to deal with any challenges that come with the adoption of new and often foreign technologies. Dependence on foreign technology and expertise can hinder local innovation and self-sufficiency, perpetuating a cycle of dependency. ClassDojo, if not curated properly, can perpetuate power imbalances and hinder genuine autonomy in formerly colonized nations. Additionally, as ClassDojo targets the most vulnerable, our children, and schools, the core process of culture and development, it is well situated to perpetuate the dominance of Western culture. Unfortunately, the adoption of ClassDojo in the classrooms of many Muslim majority countries is proceeding rapidly without any due consideration to these issues. This has serious implications regarding the self-actualization of Muslims in their homelands.

Corporate led educational reform

Is the classroom environment truly safe for our children? Some view ClassDojo's quantification of students' behavior and social interactions to achieve classroom compliance as a form of discipline and intimidation and not necessarily as positive and conducive to learning.[43] They view it as a form of corporate-led educational reform that ultimately profits large businesses. What kind of critical attitude should we have when we are allowing our children to be subjected to the datafication of their behaviors and social interactions in the classroom? Educators, as reflective practitioners, as they deploy new technologies in the classroom, must critically examine the impact of those technologies and ask why do we look for certain patterns in these piles of data, in whose interests, and for what purposes?

What happens when ClassDojo's data is used by AI and machine learning?

AI and machine learning depend significantly on data for their training and enhancement. These technologies process large datasets to identify patterns and make predictions, frequently surpassing human abilities. The ability of AI to comprehend and manipulate data has the potential to drive breakthroughs across multiple fields. AI and machine learning have the potential to transform teaching and learning by making it more efficient, personalized, and responsive to the needs of students and teachers.

AI and machine learning can individualize lessons to align with students' needs and preferences. They can analyze student performance and provide real-time feedback and help identify where support is needed the most. Via predictive analysis they can identify at-risk students by analyzing patterns in data, enabling early interventions. They can also enhance accessibility for students with disabilities. More and more educators are exploring the potential of AI in education. It is only a matter of time that data generated by educational apps such as ClassDojo will eventually be used by AI and machine learning in the schooling of our children, not only to provide individualized learning experiences but also in the formation of policy.

What are the risks of using AI and machine learning in education? Both rely heavily on data; therefore, the effectiveness of any conclusions or actions informed by AI and machine learning will depend on the quality of the data. AI systems can perpetuate existing biases if trained on flawed datasets, leading to unfair treatment or inaccurate assessments of problems and challenges we are trying to find solutions to. Since ClassDojo is clearly built on the secular worldview, any data generated by it will be biased and its analysis will lead to further perpetuate that worldview. The over-reliance on such technologies can widen the digital divide. It can lead to a loss in human interaction as students may turn more and more to AI for answers. This may impact the development of social and emotional skills.

Since the AI systems are based purely on quantifiable data, it will not be able to provide the holistic approach to learning and development that is part of the Islamic ethos. Islam provides a specific understanding of God and the unseen world, but both are transcendent and beyond human comprehension; therefore, cannot be quantified. From an Islamic perspective AI systems will always be limited in their approach to teaching and learning.

Data Surveillance and Data Analytics

Social media apps collect user data, often without the user's awareness, to identify patterns of conduct or activities to predict future behavior.[29] Data surveillance or dataveillance is a form of continuous surveillance using metadata. It differs from traditional surveillance in a keyway: while surveillance typically involves monitoring for specific purposes, dataveillance involves the ongoing tracking of (meta)data for unspecified predefined purposes. In this sense, it is more invasive than surveillance and penetrates every fiber of our social fabric. Some have compared this to using a thermometer to measure the feverish symptoms of crowds reacting to social or natural events. Information scientists, like meteorologists, use these patterns of online social behavior to predict future actions. It is the science of "life mining" where the collective digital trails left behind by people are used to extract "useful" knowledge to not only predict future behavior but also to shape it.[29]

Behavioral Surveillance

ClassDojo integrates behaviorist reward systems with behavioral monitoring to subtly influence and modify children's classroom behaviors. Some have criticized it as a system of awarding "virtual badges of obedience" that reinforces particular norms of contested behaviors.[5] ClassDojo constantly collects real-time data on observable behaviors. It allows teachers to display students' progress alongside each other encouraging behavioral competition and group surveillance. It also shares this data in real-time with parents enabling them to inspect and police their child's progress. It is an efficient behaviorist surveillance machine and part of the persuasive technologies that are aligned with psycho-policies that have authorized state-sanctioned surveillance across the public sector globally.[44]

The continuous surveillance of student behavior puts children on edge and under undue stress. Muslim children are taught from a young age that Allah ﷻ watches us all the time. We are told that we are assigned two angels, *kiraaman kaatibin*, who write down all our good and bad deeds. However, there is a stark difference between the continuous surveillance of children's behavior in ClassDojo and the continuous Divine surveillance of our life. Divine surveillance is done by Allah ﷻ who is the Compassionate, the All Forgiving and the All Merciful and He ﷻ has kept the door of *tawbah* open for all who wish to turn back to Him ﷻ. This knowledge gives us hope despite the awareness that we are under the continuous watch of Allah ﷻ. The same cannot be said of the digital surveillance of our lives. Not only can we not compare those who have access to our data to Allah's Mercy and Forgiveness, we cannot guarantee the sincerity of their motives.

Psychological Surveillance

ClassDojo focuses on monitoring psychological traits and implementing interventions aimed at changing attitudes, beliefs, and personality, particularly by promoting positive emotions. In this way, it introduces new forms of psycho-policy within education. The strong connection between ClassDojo and emerging governmental priorities related to children's social and emotional well-being reflects a modern intertwining of psychological expertise, commercial educational technology, and policy goals, resulting in a fast-tracking of government behavior change initiatives in schools.

ClassDojo applies new psychological and neuroscientific concepts, such as the growth mindsets, emerging from Stanford University's PERTS lab. It treats classroom behaviors technocratically where pathways to solutions are sought by increased data on behavior. Such a reductionist approach is at odds with the holistic approach to child development in Islam. Therefore, Islamic schools, if wanting to use ClassDojo, must do so with a well articulated implementation plan that negotiates the gaps and the negative impact of implementing such an invasive and persuasive technology in the tarbiyah of their students. This implementation plan should include training for teachers on the critical use of ClassDojo.

Erosion of social trust

The public puts faith in the institutions handling of their data by the rules set by publicly accountable agents. Ethical commitments to user data by tech giants like Facebook and Google are highly superficial. They have based their social contract with people on transparency, requiring authentic and verifiable personal information from users; however, they offer little transparency in return. Many of these companies remain engaged in legal battles to defend their continuously changing *Terms of Use* that keep stretching their privacy policy. Additionally, as the Snowden documents made clear and later the journalists found out, government agencies and businesses routinely test their legal limits and do break the rules.[29] More significantly, the Snowden files have heightened awareness of the interconnected practices among government intelligence, businesses, and academia in adopting the ideological foundations of dataism.

The credibility of the whole ecosystem of connective media is problematic and we need to question the roles of government, corporations, and academia in handling our data. Academics play a key role in fostering social trust. Academic institutions often serve as key authority in determining what is considered fact versus opinion, and what qualifies as fact versus speculation. The lines between facts, opinions, and predictions, as well as between objectivity, subjectivity, and potentiality are increasingly blurred as human behavior is encoded in (meta)data and shaped by platforms and as predictive analytics and real-time data analytics become the preferred modes of scientific analysis of human behavior.[29] Educators must learn and teach students to disentangle this mixture of facts and opinions that has become our usual diet of information if we want to live authentic lives.

Soft tech companies, governments, and academia are co-developing data mining projects, albeit for different purposes. While soft tech may primarily be collecting data to make more money, governments may be doing so for intelligence purposes, whereas academia sees Big Data as the new frontier in research. Their interests converge in various ways and complement each other. For example, Microsoft collaborated with the C.I.A on Project Chess with the goal of making mined data from Skype calls accessible to law enforcement.[45] The problem here is the faith we seem to place in high-tech companies and government agencies regarding the protection of our data from exploitation. This blind trust in the objectivity of the data itself and in the integrity of institutions using data mining methods forms a core component of dataism. However, all these organizations are intimately interconnected within the same ecosystem, making it very difficult to maintain neutrality in the management of user data.

Muslims have experienced government surveillance and Islamophobia post-9/11 and matters related to data privacy are deeply concerning to them. Police and intelligence services have used social media data to forecast terrorist activities. The Muslim community has often been judged, mistreated, and demonized based on this non-representative data; just a few percentages of Muslims from a certain age group actively use social media. There is a real fear of how data of Muslim children from ClassDojo can be manipulated to "control" the future of Muslims.

Surveillance Capitalism

We live in an age of surveillance capitalism where our personal information has become a commodity that can be bought and sold, often without our knowledge.[46] Companies and businesses collect vast amounts of data, often without our explicit consent, through various means like tracking online activities, monitoring social media interactions, and using smart devices. Companies then use this data to tailor advertisements and to shape products, services, and even social norms.

There are many "salah apps" that provide a valuable service to Muslims regarding their obligatory duty to pray five times a day. Many of these apps work by collecting user data. An analysis of 50 Islamic prayer apps found that almost all of them share data with third-party services such as advertisers.[47] There were allegations against the popular prayer timing app Muslim Pro and the dating app Muslim Mingle of selling user data to third party data brokers that eventually landed in the hands of the US military.[47] Though Muslim Pro dismissed these allegations as untrue, it further eroded Muslim trust in social media apps and was followed by mass deletion of the app. Muslim leaders and community members weighed in on the scandal calling it a betrayal of Muslims.

Surveillance capitalism is driven by those in power preying on dependent populations who are unaware of the many ways they are being tapped into for data collection. Therefore, data collection by its very nature, is a manipulative act inclined towards the exploitation of the many by the few. This gap continues to increase with the same level of acceleration as developments in connectivity across Internet technologies.

ClassDojo is one of the many instances of surveillance capitalism where children's behavior data is mined in exchange for free services that facilitate some of the core functions of a school, communication and student discipline. One of the main purposes of surveillance capitalism is to mine behavioral data to understand and predict future behavior. ClassDojo has literally tapped into the motherlode of all behavioral data, children's behavior!

ClassDojo intends to generate revenue by selling media content and premium features to teachers and schools.[5] Its global reach has allowed it to collect massive amounts of significant data about children and teachers. It is well positioned to sell this data to government agencies and schools who will find it valuable in measuring the impact of their programs (especially the new psychological goals and organizational behavior) and in rating schools. It is well positioned to influence the existing political structures and accountability systems in the educational landscape.

Consumer data theft

Consumer data privacy has become a significant concern of our times with the widespread theft of consumer data. Cyberattacks have increased with sophisticated hacking techniques making it easier for criminals to access sensitive user data. More entry points are available for these criminals with the proliferation of Internet of Things devices as many of them have weak security protocols. The business model of many companies is built on selling user data to third parties. It is difficult for users to keep track of how their data is handled and secured by these third-party buyers.

Teaching students to be safe online

Teachers should actively teach students to safeguard their privacy and security online. The following skillsets should be taught to students as soon as they are able to use technology on their own:

- *Password management:* Teach students how to create strong passwords, use password managers, and setup two-factor authentication.

- *Identifying phishing and scam attempts:* teach students how to identify suspicious emails, messages, and phone calls.

- *Safe browsing habits:* Students should be trained in safe browsing habits such as using HTTPS, avoiding public Wi-Fi for sensitive transactions, and clearing browser history and cookies periodically.

- *Social media privacy settings:* Teach students how to set up the privacy settings on social media apps, etc. to protect their personal information. Also, train them not to overshare information.

- *Understanding data privacy laws and rights:* Students should be introduced to privacy laws and should know what their rights are under these laws. They should be trained on the idea of consent and should be able to find out what information they are providing access to when consenting.

- *Protecting devices and networks:* Students should know how to update the software on their devices, use antivirus and anti-malware software, and understand the importance of using secure networks.

- *Ethical digital footprint management:* Teach students that whatever we do is recorded by Allah ﷻ. Also relate this to how everything we do online leaves a digital footprint that can be traced. Muslims should always act with *ihsan*, as if they are seeing Allah ﷻ and if unable to do so then at least Allah ﷻ is seeing them. Additionally, we should practice the Golden Rule, treat others better than they would treat us and always wish well for others and do not harm them.

- *Critical consumer of media:* train students in becoming a critical consumer of media and information. Concepts of *halal* and *haram*, being safe online, and mutual respect will keep them safe.

Data Mining

We live in an age where data is considered the most valuable resource, more valuable than oil or gold.[48] Digital platforms are developed with the primary purpose of data mining. Even on e-commerce platforms, businesses view selling data as more lucrative than buying and selling items. Many apps and social media platforms rely on this model to offer free services to consumers and care more about gathering user data than securing it. Therefore, privacy of consumer data is not a primary concern for many high-tech companies and understandably has not kept pace with the many technological advancements.

ClassDojo has faced scrutiny regarding data privacy practices, particularly concerning how it collects and uses data from students and teachers. While it provides tools for classroom management and communication, concerns have been raised about potential data mining and the ways that user information might be analyzed or shared. It's essential to review their privacy policy and terms of service to understand how they handle data and what measures are in place to protect user privacy.

According to Islam, data privacy is a fundamental right that should be upheld collectively.[48] There is an urgent need to secure customer data. Effective cybersecurity measures must be put in place to ensure Islamic principles of *amanah* (trust) are maintained. These security measures should be rooted in the Islamic heritage regarding privacy and be able to rearticulate the historical positions regarding privacy in light of new socio-technological developments.

Surveillance of Muslims in an age of Islamophobia

The sensationalized and negative portrayal of Muslims in news and entertainment has contributed to the rise in Islamophobia. Politicians and influencers have used online platforms to spread anti-Muslim rhetoric to legitimize Islamophobia in public discourse. Social media and online platforms have spread misinformation about Islam and Muslims, reinforcing negative stereotypes and misconceptions. Algorithms on social media create echo chambers filled with hate speech and derogatory comments about Muslims normalizing and amplifying

Islamophobic sentiments. Many Muslims and communities face targeted harassment and trolling online and live in a culture of fear and isolation.

The Muslim community has primarily been reactive in fighting back Islamophobia. Most Muslim civil rights organizations are busy responding to hate incidents and discrimination in the workplace, etc. We need to take proactive measures to change the discourse on Islam and Muslims. The Muslims in Canada Data Initiative (MiCDI), established by the Institute of Islamic Studies, University of Toronto, Mississauga, and the Sociology Department seems to be one such initiative that was formed to provide factual information about the Muslim community in order to correct stereotypes and to remove any barriers.[49] They examine and develop large-scale data sets to improve the visibility of Muslims across Canada and to inform policy and decisions that impact Muslims. More initiatives like the MiCDI are needed to bring Muslim voices to the forefront to combat Islamophobia.

Indoctrinating students into a culture of surveillance

ClassDojo, like other industries is using data filtering and algorithmic manipulation for commercial reasons. It is indoctrinating students into a culture of surveillance where metadata is the currency that is being exchanged in return for communication services and security.[2, 43] Children can customize their avatars only if they have a ClassDojo account and parental consent for ClassDojo's collection, use, and disclosure of their information (I can imagine the second grader in our school pestering her parents to consent so she can customize her avatar).[41] Parents often do not consider where and how the collected data might eventually be used. Government agencies can purchase this service from ClassDojo if they see it as essential for education in exchange for protecting children's data; however, they are allowing such unequal transactions to take place right under their noses. People are becoming more and more comfortable with this Faustian bargain and children are being trained from a very early age to view this as the norm in their societies.

Since March 2016, ClassDojo has enabled "school-wide" features to allow whole schools to sign up for an account.[5] Teachers and leaders can "safely" share photos, videos, and messages with all parents connected to the school at once. In the Fall of 2024, ClassDojo also introduced school wide points. ClassDojo also has a paid version with a 7-day free trial period for parents, called ClassDojo Plus, that enables parents to give "home points" to manage children's behavior at home. All this creep positions ClassDojo as a behavioral surveillance platform that extends beyond the classroom walls.

Constant surveillance of children can lead to anxiety and stress. The pressure to always "perform" in front of peers, teachers, and parents can lead to heightened stress. This may stifle creativity and risk-taking, as children may fear negative points for making mistakes and stepping outside expected norms. All of this can seriously impact their self-esteem and self-efficacy. Redirection of children must be done compassionately, discreetly, and meaningfully. This is the sunnah of the Prophet ﷺ.

Notions of privacy in Islam

The cybersecurity and data privacy landscape is rapidly evolving. It is important for Muslims to understand how Islamic principles and values intersect with contemporary cybersecurity practices. There is a need for inclusive and culturally aligned approaches to cybersecurity that is informed by a deep understanding of Islamic ethics and jurisprudence. Muslim scholars have distinctly marked the private versus the public sphere and took measures to safeguard the private sphere as enshrined in the Qur'an and the Sunnah.[50] There was a significant paradigm shift among the early classical scholars (first 2 centuries of AH) and late classical scholars (3-13 centuries of AH) in Islamic thought about privacy where notions of privacy shifted from narrow and rigid to broader and more flexible ones.[50]

The shift in privacy laws where the early scholars focused more on physical dwellings was due to the rapid urbanization Muslim communities experienced as Islam spread rapidly across many lands. This led to a massive social transformation across the *ummah*. In a very short period, people who had lived a nomadic life, free to move about, and surrounded by large spaces suddenly found themselves confined to small spaces in densely populated cities with many other strangers. Their private space became suddenly very restricted. Notions of privacy became intimately tied with the physical spaces people were living in, which came to be represented by the house they lived in. Thus, conceptions of privacy were based on property rights. As Muslim life became more urbanized and complex, notions of privacy became more abstract and were extended beyond physical boundaries. Internet technologies such as social media have further disrupted our notions of privacy. We must reconceptualize our notions of privacy, as our scholars did before, to address the disruption in our privacy caused by invasive social media technologies.

The General Data Protection Regulation (GDPR) in Europe and the Health Insurance Portability and Accountability Act (HIPPA) in the US are examples of legal frameworks designed to protect individual data. There are also ethical guidelines from professional organizations like the Association for Computer Machinery that highlight the moral obligations of scientists and technologists.[51] Muslim majority countries do not have similar robust laws. Majority of these frameworks have ethical elements that align with many Islamic concepts but are based on a secular worldview that often doesn't recognize the existence of Divine authority and our consequent obligations and duties.

Muslim majority countries have attempted to safeguard the intellectual property, freedom of expression, and privacy rights of their citizens in line with moral, ethical, and religious aspects of their populations. However, power dynamics often supersede any other considerations regarding the development of related laws. Governments enact laws to ensure and maintain the hegemonic status quo and consequently, these laws violate many fundamental rights of their citizens.[48]

Many high-tech companies operate across national boundaries; however, they are not held accountable by the laws of each country. These "foreign" companies operate within a power structure that facilitates neocolonial policies. They may be primarily responsible for the laws of their host country and are able to circumvent many of the related laws in other countries. Therefore, privacy of consumer data cannot be guaranteed at the same level of confidence across national boundaries. This is primarily the case with many Muslim majority countries where theft of consumer data is much higher than in other countries.[48] Additionally, Islamophobia and the war on terrorism has put Muslims under heavy surveillance making us more vulnerable to digital manipulation and exploitation.

The lack of operationalization of Islam in everyday life is an ailment of our times where many aspects of daily living are devoid of Islamic principles and individual Muslims do not have Islamic legal frameworks to guide their daily digital activities. Islam is a way of life for more than a billion people worldwide and the principles and values in Islamic ethics and jurisprudence must be taken into consideration as they do impact individual and collective behavior in the digital world.

Privacy in Islam is not just a legal concept but also a moral one. It is considered a fundamental human right in Islam and is protected by Islamic law. Accordingly, by extension, data privacy is a fundamental right in Islam that must also be collectively maintained.[48] The Islamic principles of privacy, honesty, and protection from harm align with contemporary cybersecurity and data privacy norms. There is limited research on the legal and ethical implications of cybersecurity and data privacy from an Islamic perspective.

Concept of Privacy in the Quran

There are several verses in the Qur'an that lay down rules regarding access to residential space or private space:

Allah ﷻ in Surah Al-Noor orders us not to enter houses other than our own without seeking permission until and unless it is a facility that is open to public access:

يَٰٓأَيُّهَا ٱلَّذِينَ ءَامَنُوا۟ لَا تَدْخُلُوا۟ بُيُوتًا غَيْرَ بُيُوتِكُمْ حَتَّىٰ تَسْتَأْنِسُوا۟ وَتُسَلِّمُوا۟ عَلَىٰٓ أَهْلِهَا ذَٰلِكُمْ

خَيْرٌ لَّكُمْ لَعَلَّكُمْ تَذَكَّرُونَ (٢٧) فَإِن لَّمْ تَجِدُوا۟ فِيهَآ أَحَدًا فَلَا تَدْخُلُوهَا حَتَّىٰ يُؤْذَنَ لَكُمْ

وَإِن قِيلَ لَكُمُ ٱرْجِعُوا۟ فَٱرْجِعُوا۟ هُوَ أَزْكَىٰ لَكُمْ وَٱللَّهُ بِمَا تَعْمَلُونَ عَلِيمٌ (٢٨) لَّيْسَ عَلَيْكُمْ

جُنَاحٌ أَن تَدْخُلُوا۟ بُيُوتًا غَيْرَ مَسْكُونَةٍ فِيهَا مَتَٰعٌ لَّكُمْ وَٱللَّهُ يَعْلَمُ مَا تُبْدُونَ وَمَا تَكْتُمُونَ (٢٩)

O you who believe! Do not enter homes other than your own, until you have asked permission and greeted their occupants. That is better for you, that you may be aware. And if you find no one in them, do not enter them until you are given permission. And if it is said to you, "Turn back," then turn back. That is more proper for you. Allah is aware of what you do. There is no blame on you for entering uninhabited houses, in which are belongings of yours. Allah knows what you reveal and what you conceal. (Quran 24:27-29).

The above verses come immediately after a Divine assessment of the slander against the wife of Prophet Muhammad ﷺ to cleanse society of the existing sexually charged atmosphere that resulted in the pervasion of calumny against such a noble person.[52] This prohibition came with other laws and guidance that discouraged free mixing of the sexes together, forbidding women to appear in their make up before other *non-mahram* men (and eventually the *hijab*), banning prostitution, and encouraging men and women to get married at the earliest for these are the causes that lead to rise in sensuality in society. It was this sexually charged atmosphere that inclined people to readily participate in any real or fictitious scandal. This is the Divine comprehensive approach to reform that Allah ﷻ takes in curbing the spread of evil in society instead of just forbidding an evil or punishing the offender. It is important that we extend such comprehensive reforms in our digital age where the spreading of such scandals have become the currency for garnering more likes on our social media.

The above verses also underline the need of consent in privacy.[48] People must be granted permission from the residents of the house to enter it; otherwise, they are prohibited from doing so. Likewise, companies, governments, and individuals must obtain permission from users to access their data. Additionally, verse 12 in Surah Al-Hujurat also restricts people from excessive suspicion, spying, and slandering:

يَـٰٓأَيُّهَا ٱلَّذِينَ ءَامَنُوا۟ ٱجْتَنِبُوا۟ كَثِيرًا مِّنَ ٱلظَّنِّ إِنَّ بَعْضَ ٱلظَّنِّ إِثْمٌ وَلَا تَجَسَّسُوا۟ وَلَا يَغْتَب بَّعْضُكُم بَعْضًا أَيُحِبُّ أَحَدُكُمْ أَن يَأْكُلَ لَحْمَ أَخِيهِ مَيْتًا فَكَرِهْتُمُوهُ وَٱتَّقُوا۟ ٱللَّهَ إِنَّ ٱللَّهَ تَوَّابٌ رَّحِيمٌ (١٢)

Believers, avoid being excessively suspicious, for some suspicion is a sin. Do not spy, nor backbite one another. Would any of you like to eat the flesh of his dead brother? You would surely detest it. Have fear of Allah. Surely Allah is inclined to accept repentance, is Most Compassionate. (Quran 49:12).

From the verses in Surah Nur and Surah Hujurat, we can conclude that in Islam the concept of privacy is inextricably linked to morality. Ethical behavior is required from Muslims to protect data privacy.

How the Prophet ﷺ established privacy in the early Muslim community

The Prophet ﷺ when implementing the commandment revealed in the verses cited above did not just understand it as a restriction to entry in houses but extended this concept of privacy where it was forbidden to peep into a house and even to read another person's letter without permission.[53] For example, Abu Daud reports in his hadith collection that Abdullah ibn Abbas ﷺ reports that the Prophet ﷺ said: "Whoever glances through the letter of his brother without his permission, glances into fire."[52] The Prophet ﷺ modeled this commandment in his demeanor and behavior and in his ﷺ relationships with others thereby redirecting them to the proper ways of respecting each other's privacy. Those around him ﷺ started emulating him until it became the norm in Al-Madinah.

Occupancy based privacy

In Islam, the concept of privacy is closely related to occupancy, i.e. a facility that is regularly inhabited by people remains inaccessible to the public even if it is non-residential.[53] People enjoy free access only to regularly unoccupied facilities. However, the presence of a lawful occupant (owner, guest, or tenant) justifies entrance-restrictions and protects the place from outsiders.

Isti'nas and greeting before entering a place

Allah ﷻ in the verses in Surah Al-Nur (Quran 24:27) asks us to make *isti'nas* (announcing one's presence) and to *tusallimu* (greet) to initiate the process of seeking permission into a place. Ibn Abbas ﷺ held that the correct reading of *isti'nas* is *isti'dhan* (announcing) after which we should clearly request for permission to enter.[50] This can be a cough or a gentle sound to notify the inhabitants of our presence and to let them know that we wish to enter.

The Prophet ﷺ modeled these behaviors for others. He would correct people when they did not observe these rules and procedures for entering dwellings. Some of these hadiths include

وعن أبي موسى الأشعري رضي الله عنه قال: قال رسول الله صلى الله عليه وسلم : " الاستئذان ثلاث، فإن أذن لك وإلا فارجع" ((متفق عليه))

Abu Musa Al-Ash'ari ﷺ reported: The Messenger of Allah ﷺ said, "Permission is to be sought thrice. If permission is granted, you may enter; otherwise, go back". Reported in Al- Bukhari and Muslim.[54]

وعن سهل بن سعد قال: قال رسول الله صلى الله عليه وسلم : "إنما جعل الاستئذان من أجل البصر" ((متفق عليه)).

Sahl bin Sa'd ﷺ reported: The Messenger of Allah ﷺ said, "Seeking permission to enter (somebody's house) has been prescribed in order to restrain the eyes (from looking at something we are not supposed to look at)." Reported in Al-Bukhari and Muslim and Riyad as-Salihin 871.[55]

وعن ربعي بن حراش قال: حدثنا رجل من بني عامر استأذن على النبي صلى الله عليه وسلم وهو في بيت، فقال: ألج؟ فقال رسول الله صلى الله عليه وسلم لخادمه: "أخرج إلى

هذا وعلمه الاستئذان، فقل له: قل: السلام عليكم، أأدخل؟" فسمعه الرجل فقال: السلام عليكم، أأدخل؟ فأذن له النبي صلى الله عليه وسلم، فدخل. ((رواه أبو داود بإسناد صحيح)).

Rib'i bin Hirash ﷺ reported: A man of Banu 'Amir tribe has told us that he had asked the Prophet ﷺ for permission to enter when he was at home. He said: "May I enter?" the Messenger of Allah ﷺ said to the servant, "Go out and instruct him about the manner of seeking permission. Tell him to say: As-Salamu 'Alaikum (may peace be upon you). May I come in?" The man heard this and said: "As-Salamu 'Alaikum (may peace be upon you). May I come in?" The Prophet ﷺ then granted him permission and he entered. Reported in Abu Dawud and Riyad as-Salihin 872.[55]

These new rules and procedures came at a time when most houses did not have doors, and many didn't even have curtains to cover the entrances. It set a new precedent in Al-Madinah, creating safe personal spaces for individuals, protecting their honor and dignity. This had a significant impact on the law and order in the entire city. People started valuing each other and started recognizing the rights of others over them and their rights over others.

The principle of awrah and data privacy

The idea of *awrah* (عورة) in Islamic tradition pertains to the importance of personal space and privacy, and this concept can be adapted to the digital age. *Awrah* has two meanings:[50, 53]

1. The first one relates to physical modesty and denotes those body parts that a believer must conceal from others. The criteria for *awrah* are different for men and women and for adults and children. It varies on the type of relationship one has with another person (*mahram* vs. *non-mahram*) and is contextually

defined (one's own home vs. another person's home vs. a public space). The Islamic dress code and social interaction are based on this.

2. The second concept of *awrah* relates to what we wish to keep out of public reach. This varies from person to person and is dependent on what we deem as private and what we wish to share. This also relates to the Islamic concepts of *ghibah* (backbiting) and *namimah* (slander), which are considered major sins in Islam. The Quran and hadith view them as harmful to both the individual and the community. They emphasize the seriousness of these sins and discourage us from it and encourage us to speak kindly and protect each other's honor. Exposing any information that an individual considers to be private (as part of his *awrah*) can constitute a sin in Islam. It is *ghibah* if it is true and it is *namimah* if it is a lie about that individual.

Some Muslim jurists, based on the concept of *awrah*, extended the concept of privacy to people's desire for privacy and what they considered to be private and sensitive information.[50] This extends the concept of privacy beyond the privacy of the home to other domains of public life. This impacts the concept of privacy in cyberspace as well. Private information in today's digital age must be accorded the same level of legal protection as accorded in the past by Muslim scholars to sensitive information.

The concept of *awrah* sanctifies personal space and privacy and guides us to respect each other's privacy and dignity in our interactions with others. We can apply these principles in cyberspace to protect personal information and to define and respect digital boundaries. They can also guide organizations handling of personal information with care and integrity. Thus, the concept of *awrah* can serve as a moral framework to ensure and maintain privacy in the digital age.

Private space has significantly reduced in the digital world we live in and there is a desire for temporary solitude that must be respected. People now pay good money to vacation in dead spots where no radio/electronic signal can penetrate. The Islamic concepts on privacy can be used to find the peace and solitude we seek in our busy and digitally driven lives.

Khalwa (خلوة) ï The sanctity of private space

Classical Islamic scholars extended the notion of "protected entities" from beyond the physical objects (houses, etc.) to the mental sphere.[50] They equated the "house" mentioned in the verses in Surah Al-Nur in the Qur'an as a space that provides us with solitude, *khalwa*. In Islam, the concept of *khalwa* refers to a state of seclusion or isolation meant for a spiritual retreat. In *khalwa*, we isolate ourselves from social interactions to focus on our relationship with Allah ﷻ. It creates a space that is meant for personal meditation, prayer, study, reflection and contemplation, and allows us to deepen our spirituality and to connect profoundly with our Creator ﷻ.

Also, Muslims are required not to be in *khalwa* with the *nonmahram* opposite gender to avoid temptation and to maintain modesty. Classical Muslim scholars viewed *khalwa* as a space where we can conduct our private and domestic affairs freely without any intrusion from others. They envisioned a place where we can escape for moments of complete peace of mind and a location where we can act freely even if those actions violate legal norms.

We are in desperate need of creating spaces for solitude and reflection amid the constant connectivity of modern technology. The constant connectivity to the outside world and the consequent continuous invasion of privacy has disrupted our peace of mind. Applying the concept of *khalwa* to the digital world will enable us to create such intentional spaces where peace of mind can be restored. It can also help us to establish clear boundaries regarding online interactions with the opposite gender to maintain modesty, mutual respect, and honor. By observing the concepts of *khalwa*, we can foster a sense of seclusion and spiritual focus within the continuously disconcerting digital landscape.

Why is privacy so important for Muslims in the digital age?

In Islam, privacy was protected to establish a pious and God-conscious community.[50] People are prone to suspicion. Therefore, the Quran has taken extra precaution to protect the privacy of the individual's home to protect the reputation of individuals. Individual privacy is safeguarded to protect the reputation of the Muslim. We are held accountable by society and the legal system for our public behavior, but we are to be left alone and judged by Allah ﷻ for our sins committed in privacy as long as those sins do not impact another individual. This doesn't mean that private space is neglected; rather, it is dealt in detail in the Quran where Muslims are constantly reminded to always observe *taqwa* and specially in one's privacy (see the Quran, Surah Mulk). This creates a stage for the concept of *taqwa* to be practiced and developed in a safe environment without any harm to others.

Muslim scholars viewed securing the sanctity of the individual space as instrumental in establishing a stable community. Early Muslim scholars protected domestic privacy even when the inhabitants of a house were committing a sin and did not allow outsiders with a license to invade the house.[50] We feel safe and motivated to participate in society if we are assured that no one will trespass upon our individual space and be subjected to social punishment. If we are constantly monitored and scrutinized by authorities and those around us, then we will retreat and restrict our social contacts to a minimum to survive. Therefore, Islam has taken great care to provide this sense of security to the individual in his/her private space without any public interference. In this safe space, the believer is only accountable to his/her Creator ﷻ.

The cyberworld has disrupted many of our personal spaces. So how does this concept of occupancy-based privacy extend to cyberspaces? Sins committed in cyberspace infiltrate the very confines of our homes and spread on a global scale; therefore, must be stopped.

There are different cultural norms regarding privacy and security. Some cultures may prioritize individual privacy over collective security; whereas, other cultures may prioritize the opposite. Children though are a protected population in most cultures/countries and their privacy and security is carefully guarded. How does ClassDojo disrupt the privacy and security of children's data collected?

When we start invading the privacy of our students' behavior via ClassDojo then we are reducing that safe space for them to learn from their mistakes and to practice their *taqwa*. ClassDojo's ability to display student progress boards in the class and instantaneously share with parents, students' infractions breaches many of the privacy protocols established in the Qur'an. This has a detrimental impact on the development of the children because it distances them from forging a strong relationship with Allah ﷻ that is important in reformation of the self.

Concealing one's sins

Concealing one's sin that has not impacted others is encouraged in Islam. A tradition of the Prophet ﷺ states that Allah ﷻ conceals the sins of a person on the Day of Judgement and takes account of the person's sins in private if he/she concealed them in this world:

عَنْ أَبِي هُرَيْرَةَ قَالَ قَالَ رَسُولُ اللَّهِ صَلَّى اللَّهُ عَلَيْهِ وَسَلَّمَ كُلُّ أُمَّتِي مُعَافًى إِلَّا الْمُجَاهِرِينَ وَإِنَّ مِنَ الْمُجَاهَرَةِ أَنْ يَعْمَلَ الرَّجُلُ بِاللَّيْلِ عَمَلًا ثُمَّ يُصْبِحَ وَقَدْ سَتَرَهُ اللَّهُ عَلَيْهِ فَيَقُولَ يَا فُلَانُ عَمِلْتُ الْبَارِحَةَ كَذَا وَكَذَا وَقَدْ بَاتَ يَسْتُرُهُ رَبُّهُ وَيُصْبِحُ يَكْشِفُ سِتْرَ اللَّهِ عَنْهُ

Abu Huraira ﷺ reported: The Messenger of Allah ﷺ said, "Everyone from my nation will be forgiven except those who sin in public. Among them is a man who commits an evil deed in the night that Allah has hidden for him, then in the morning he says: O people, I have committed this sin! His Lord had hidden it during the night, but in the morning, he reveals what Allah has hidden." Reported in Ṣaḥīḥ al-Bukhārī 6069 and Ṣaḥīḥ Muslim 2990.[56]

Maintaining privacy is very important for the moral development of the individual and society. In fact, Muslim scholars encouraged reporting a transgressor who misbehaves in public without any conscience about his misconduct being discovered and takes lightly that people are watching him. Such a person destroys the laws of the land but also the moral fabric of society, a greater sin than the misconduct itself! In such a case, punishing the sinner becomes a deterrent to sinners from revealing their own sin. On the other hand, Al-Ghazali instructs a believer engaged in "forbidding wrong," not to investigate misconduct performed behind "closed doors".[50] This is to minimize the impact of the wrong on the society. What happens when children's misconduct gets put on public display within the classroom as in ClassDojo or gets shared with parents instantaneously? How does that impact the moral upbringing of the child? Does it make the child think that since a lot of students misbehave daily it is OK to do so?

Centralizing the Islamic concept of *amanah* (trust) in data collection and privacy

Islam granted individuals privacy as a basic right more than 1400 years ago. Enshrined in the Islamic concept of *amanah* (أمانة), individual privacy is a core concept in the Islamic judicial system. Recently, some Muslims in high-tech have highlighted the importance of preserving the privacy of data collected by connecting it to the concept of *amanah*, a sacred duty expected of every Muslim.[47] They are trying to balance between building something useful for the Muslim community, like a salah app, without infringing on anyone's right to privacy.

Muslim tech entrepreneurs, who consider user privacy as an *amanah* between them and the community, are seeking ways to preserve the privacy of Muslims. One such app is Pillars that was launched in April 2021 and claims to not share any user data with third party services by making sure the data is stored only on the user's device. However, creators of such apps find it extremely difficult to continue to maintain data privacy in an ecosystem that facilitates dataveillance practices.

Maintaining *amanah* within the Muslim communities by ensuring data privacy is maintained requires extensive collaboration across community members. For example, developers of Salah Space, the app used to reserve a spot for salah in the local masjid during COVID-19, had to engage Muslim lawyers, Islamic scholars, community leaders, and members of the Muslim community as they were developing privacy solutions that satisfied the needs of the developers as well as maintained the privacy of users.[47] Some Muslim activists view even such efforts as insufficient and advocate for greater transparency such as asking developers to make the app fully open source so the code could be audited by anyone.

Muslim scholars must reconceptualize our notions of privacy once again as we now live in a hybrid world made up of physical and cyber spaces. This hybrid world has further restricted private space and new interpretations of the Islamic law are needed to preserve the sanctity of private space given by the Qur'an. This is needed to once again make our houses sanctuaries free of human censorship in which we are only accountable to Allah ﷻ alone.

Online Safety with Cybersecurity Literacy

It has become increasingly difficult for users to resist platforms' privacy policies and surveillance tactics and to gain insights into the systems' interdependence and complexity. Consequently, cyberspace is an insecure and high-risk environment for all and specially for Muslims. There is a need for digital literacy to maintain privacy and security in online environments. The public must also be trained in how to negotiate the social contracts that are being dictated by connective media and the consequent restructuring of our societies.

Strategies to increase online security and privacy are not enough to mitigate such a threatening environment. Users must also receive education in the best cyber security practices and moral and ethical training that can develop mindsets that are able to guide their online choices and behavior to ensure and maintain their online safety. Many apps have a process in place for reporting abuse and cyberbullying. For example, ClassDojo maintains guidelines on acceptable behavior and violations of these rules. ClassDojo users can report incidents of abuse or cyberbullying to ClassDojo support via the app or the website. Parents can report inappropriate messages or comments directly to the teacher or admin managing the class. Students can also report directly to the teacher and can also report any harassment to the ClassDojo support team. The app also allows administrators to manage reports of bullying or abuse occurring on the platform. Teachers and parents can also block users from their class to prevent further interactions. Creating a safer environment using the above measures requires a specific mindset and skillset that comes from rigorous training.

Islamic school educators must have a certain level of foundational literacy in cybersecurity to effectively protect their students' data. Islamic schools must also teach digital or cybersecurity literacy to Muslim children from a young age, so they are aware of online threats and know how to protect themselves from them. Educators and students must understand basic operations, security settings and built-in utilities that can enhance the security of their devices. They should be able to configure newly installed applications to increase the security of their devices. There are a growing number of apps and tools that can facilitate a safer and more secure online environment. Staff and students must have knowledge about such tools and apps and know how to access them.

The International Society for Technology in Education (ISTE) standards for students outline the following learning objectives to empower students and to enhance and maintain their online safety:[57]

- **Technology Fundamentals:** Students understand fundamental concepts of how technology works, demonstrate the ability to choose and use current technologies effectively, and are adept at thoughtfully exploring emerging technologies.
- **Digital Footprint:** Students manage their digital identity and understand the lasting impact of their online behaviors on themselves and others and make safe, legal and ethical decisions in the digital world.

- **Safeguarding Well-being:** Students safeguard their well-being by being intentional about what they do online and how much time they spend online.

- **Digital Privacy:** Students take action to protect their digital privacy on devices and manage their personal data and security while online.

Adults assume that children are tech savvy and therefore do not require training in technology skills. Children are quickly able to adopt new technology; however, they do not necessarily know how to use it safely, ethically, and effectively. The Digital Use Divide is the division between those students who can use technology effectively for creation, exploration, and critical analysis (I would also add ethically) and those who are unable to.[58] Islamic schools should integrate the above ISTE Standards for Students across the curriculum and provide opportunities for students to achieve these objectives. They should make sure they are checking all of the following boxes:

- ☐ A technology plan is in place to guide the use of technology in the school

- ☐ A curriculum map to teach technology skills across grade levels has been developed and adopted.

- ☐ Dedicated technology skills curriculum has been adopted.

- ☐ Time and space (number of periods) has been allocated to teach technology skills.

- ☐ Teachers are required to include the technology curriculum in their long-range plans.

- ☐ Teachers are required to integrate technology skills across the curriculum, and this is evident in their lesson plan.

- ☐ Assessments are used to gauge students' technology skills at important transition points during their schooling.

To achieve these learning objectives with our students, educators must themselves be adept at leveraging technology to enhance online privacy and safety. The ISTE standards for educators highlight the following knowledge and skills that can help us to prepare for this task:[59]

- **Keep Current on Research:** Stay current with research that supports improved student learning outcomes, including findings from the learning sciences.
- **Model Digital Tool Use:** Model for colleagues the identification, exploration, evaluation, curation and adoption of new digital resources and tools for learning.
- **Evaluate Resources for Credibility:** Educators foster digital literacy by encouraging curiosity, reflection, and the critical evaluation of digital resources.
- **Model Safe, Legal, Ethical Practices:** Educators mentor students in safe, legal, and ethical practices with digital tools and content.
- **Manage, Protect Data:** Educators model and promote management of personal data, digital identity, and protection of student data.

Training in Islamic knowledge and skills

In addition to the knowledge and skills listed above, students and educators should also be trained in the following from an Islamic worldview:

- Evaluation of online data and resources.
- Negotiation of the online culture with respect to the Islamic values and lifestyle.
- Islamic rules on online privacy.

- Combating Islamophobia.

The knowledge and skills listed above must be required for all students and educators in Islamic schools. We should ensure that we are fulfilling these requirements through the following:

☐ Job descriptions include technology skills as a requirement.

☐ Applicants are screened for their technology skills during the interview process.

☐ Technology skills are part of the teacher performance appraisal.

☐ Professional development is provided to all staff to develop and maintain their technological skills.

☐ Case study analysis and simulations are conducted for students to unpack the issues and challenges of the complex cyberworld.

Conclusion

In this chapter we explored the ethical and privacy concerns related to the digital world. We saw how datafication of our lives has benefits but also brings with it new challenges. Datafication further amplifies Islamophobia and other types of hostility faced by Muslims and other minority cultures. Datafication is also leading to a loss in privacy, and it is important for Muslims to evaluate these changes considering Islamic notions on privacy.

We examined some of the themes mentioned above with respect to the datafication of children's behavior via ClassDojo. We looked at some of the inherent biases present in ClassDojo and their impact on child development. It is indeed very troublesome how children are indoctrinated into a culture of surveillance via apps like ClassDojo. Teachers have an Islamic duty to respect and protect the privacy of their students. The best defense against such invasive technologies like ClassDojo is to train ourselves to a level where we become critical consumers and can comfortably negotiate our Muslim identity while living in a pluralistic, globalized, digital world. A focus on digital literacy of students and educators must be formalized in a school-wide technology plan.

4

DOES THE DIGITIZED CLASSROOM MANAGEMENT WITH CLASSDOJO ALIGN WITH THE GOALS OF TARBIYAH?

Classroom management (CM) remains one of the biggest challenges in the school environment.[60] Teachers struggle daily between managing students' behavior, covering the curriculum, and fulfilling their other professional responsibilities. Despite this, teachers receive too little training in managing disruptive behaviors in the classroom and often cite classroom management as one of high needs areas in professional development. Teachers face too many classroom management challenges and have fewer options to address them; therefore, administrators, teachers, parents, and students give top priority to classroom management.[10] Therefore, the rapid adoption of ClassDojo across schools comes as no surprise since it is a tool designed to address CM challenges and manage student behavior.

Traditionally, CM has been about methods and incentive-based motivation.**Error! Bookmark not defined.** ClassDojo has made this more organized, easier, and efficient. Teachers can use ClassDojo to address disruptive behavior or off-task behavior by deducting points as a form of punishment. They can also reward points for desirable behavior. Such CM based on behaviorist principles has been proven to be effective with younger children.[2] In this chapter, we will explore the use of ClassDojo in classroom management and the impact it has on student identity and development.

Promoting the Token Economy

A token economy is based on principles of positive reinforcement to manage student behavior where tokens are used as rewards for students who meet behavior expectations. Tokens are given each time a student displays the targeted behavior. Students can then exchange these tokens for rewards that are meaningful to them. Teachers have successfully used token economies in their classrooms to manage student behavior and research consistently shows that they effectively reduce disruptive behaviors and promote positive behaviors across a wide range of students and even improve academic skills.[61, 62]

ClassDojo is part of the trend of gaming in education that incorporates a point system to create a digital token economy. Our understanding of the impact of gamification on learners is still developing; however, several studies continue to highlight its positive impact on students. In one study, ClassDojo's point system was recognized for positively impacting student engagement.[23] In another study, ClassDojo's token economy system showed an increase in positive behavior and prevocational skills of students with Down syndrome.[62]

ClassDojo is considered an electronic behavior management program (eBMP) that utilizes behaviorist theories and applied behavior analysis.[2] Though reminiscent of a traditional token economy system, it is a fully accessible online system that can simultaneously be used by multiple users in real-time. ClassDojo's digitized token economy is time saving and more convenient than a traditional token economy. It is very portable as it can be accessed anytime on any smart device via an app making it easy to implement across different learning environments.

Comparing a paper-pencil method vs a tech integrated method for implementing a token economy system reveals certain affordances and constraints of each. For example, certain constraints of the paper-pencil method force the teacher to have conversations with the students regarding the points earned; whereas that is not necessary in ClassDojo because the technology facilitates automatic update of students' points to students and to parents. In this case, teacher discretion and professional judgement is lost. Teachers can adjust this by combining the paper-pencil method with ClassDojo, where they perhaps keep track of points using pencil and paper and then provide a weekly summary using ClassDojo.

To be effective, tokens and backup reinforcers (rewards that can be exchanged for the tokens) must serve to increase the frequency of the desired behavior. Educators should carefully choose rewards that students value, so they are motivated to earn them. An effective strategy teachers employ to ensure rewards align with students' interests and preferences is to involve students in determining the rewards.

Exchanging Points for Rewards

Teachers can set up a reward system wherein students can exchange the points earned for these rewards.[61] Teachers usually create a choice board so students can visualize how many points each reward is worth. A "shopping" schedule is created to let students know when they can exchange their points for the specified rewards.

Teachers are recommended to observe the following for the reward system to be effective:

- Conduct a student preference assessment to identify rewards that are valued by students.[63]
- There should be a mix of tangible and intangible rewards. Tangible rewards are those where points can be exchanged for certain objects such as a toy, pencil, eraser, stickers, etc. Intangible rewards are rewards such as certain classroom privileges (sitting in a special chair, five minutes flex time, etc.), positive note home, etc.
- A reward that serves to evaluate behavior or provides feedback indicating success is more effective in increasing students' sense of competency and intrinsic motivation.[64]
- Have a reinforcement schedule that matches a student's needs. Shaping a new behavior may require a more frequent reinforcement schedule and over time can be extended/delayed as the behavior gets established and can eventually be faded altogether.

Teachers can use ClassDojo to shape student behavior through an enhanced version of operant conditioning traditionally practiced by behaviorists. It focuses on the external, observable causes of human behavior and doesn't take into consideration the importance of internal thoughts and motivations that drive behavior. Overuse of such a system can trivialize the important role intention, emotion, and socialization play in student learning.

Response Cost

ClassDojo allows teachers to award as well as deduct points. This transforms the token economy into a hybrid system that includes a response cost component. Response cost is a behavioral technique in which a previously awarded stimulus, such as a point, is removed to reduce (i.e., punish) the occurrence of undesirable behavior.[61] Though punishment can be useful in decreasing problematic behaviors, it can lead to other undesirable behaviors such as being antisocial and aggressive. Therefore, it is recommended that educators use procedures to reinforce positive behavior with students who are having difficulty with them before taking away any points. This also aligns with the approach of using the least intrusive/disruptive methods to redirect student behavior. Advocates of PBIS (Positive Behavior Intervention Supports) recommend that teachers should not use a blended system and should just focus on rewarding good behaviors.

One-dimensionality of ClassDojo's approach to behavior management

Several educators have opposed token economies citing that they reduce intrinsic motivation.[62] Students typically use the least challenging means to earn the rewards. Should classroom management be reduced to a point system? ClassDojo seems to foreground this and background the more important elements of classroom management such as establishing teacher/student relationships, etc. This one-dimensional approach to student behavior management trivializes the complexity of student behavior and the many factors that contribute to it. In students' minds, their behavior becomes all about gaining and losing points. There is a real danger of students superficially interpreting any infractions they commit as simply a loss in points and moving on without really reflecting on the choices that led to their behavior and its impact on others.

Use the point system to reward groups instead of students

Some have highlighted ClassDojo's point system's potential to motivate teamwork in the classroom.[7] Perhaps one way to mitigate the negative impact of a point system on individual students is for teachers to use it to reward teams. Teachers can identify the essential teamwork skills and track them through a team "monster" instead of tracking it individually. This will also mitigate any negative impact of the token economy system on student motivation.

Choice and Reflection

Choice and reflecting on our choices are important functions of character development. These features are missing in ClassDojo.[4] Teachers should mitigate these gaps with well thought out interventions. For example, points earned from tracked student data can be displayed as graphs that can be shared with parents and students. Teachers can use these graphs to enable students to reflect on their behavior for self-regulation purposes.[61]

Reflecting on feedback is a skill that needs to be taught to students. I wonder how many students reflect deeply on the feedback they receive from their teachers for self-improvement. It can be said that ClassDojo removes the focus from this to score keeping. In a token economy system, it is more about how many points I am getting rather than about using that feedback for self-improvement. Perhaps combining this approach with a reflection sheet and an action plan where students identify concrete steps with a timeline for self-improvement can greatly enhance the use of ClassDojo in the classroom.

Reflection is essential for growth and development

Innovative educators have been found to focus more on conversation and dialogue to redirect students rather than using rules and rewards and token economy systems.[2] This approach requires more effort from teachers but is more effective and long lasting in redirecting students. The Prophet ﷺ would have taken an approach of conversation and dialogue with children rather than resorting to just a token economy. Allah ﷻ asks us to reflect deeply about our choices, our actions and the impact they have on us and on those around us. There are many instances in the Qur'an where Allah ﷻ meticulously unpacks the actions of many individuals including those of the Prophet ﷺ himself so we can reflect deeply and learn important life lessons.

For example, one of the first incidents that Allah ﷻ unpacks is that of the Prophet ﷺ frowning and turning away from the blind man who wanted to ask him a question while he was busy conversing with one of the leaders in Makkah. Allah ﷻ revealed an entire Surah in the Qur'an to redirect the Prophet ﷺ and to draw upon important life lessons so he ﷺ doesn't repeat it again (see Quran Chapter 80). Such life lessons guided the interactions between the companions of the Prophet ﷺ.

ClassDojo, with its token economy, backgrounds reflection of one's actions. It is important that teachers provide opportunities for students to reflect on their actions so they can learn from them. Any student infraction must not be reduced to just a point deduction. Instead, they are teachable moments that teachers can capitalize on to teach valuable life lessons.

Likewise, behavior specific praise is important in reinforcing positive behavior in students. When that praise is reduced to the awarding of numbers (points) then it misses on the opportunity to reinforce positive behavior in meaningful ways. It is important to teach students how to use the feedback from ClassDojo productively. I wonder how many teachers take the time to do this. Or do we just stop short of score keeping?

Shaping student achievement goal orientation

In one study researchers assessed the impact of the token economy system on student achievement goal orientation between three different math classes over a period of six weeks.[2] The classes were setup as follows:

- *Class 1-Token economy group:* Used token economy in which student received tokens for getting a "B" or above grade in class assignments. They could exchange these tokens for tangible rewards.

- *Class 2-Contingency contract group:* Used a contingency contract in which students met weekly with researchers to discuss weekly goals and received gold stars and verbal praise for attaining them. However, they did not receive any tokens that could be exchanged for rewards.

- *Class 3-The control group:* Researchers met with students while they wrote out weekly goals, but no feedback or rewards were provided.

When researchers categorized the students' weekly goals as either learning-oriented goals or performance-oriented goals, they found that the token economy group (Class 1) set significantly more performance-oriented goals than learning goals, whereas the contingency contract group (Class 2) set significantly more learning goals. The control group (Class 3) set relatively equal number of performance and learning goals. This study showed that teachers should use a contingency contract with verbal feedback to motivate students towards learning-oriented values and use a token economy to motivate students towards performance-oriented values.

The point system promotes helicopter parenting

The option to notify parents in real-time of any points gained or lost takes away students' privacy and independence. Just knowing how to "break the news" to my parents used to be an important life skill but now students are deprived of this as their parents know instantly what is happening regarding their behavior even before they come home. Students' opportunity to reflect (rationalize and contextualize) on their school behavior before breaking the "bad" news to parents is lost with the point notification system.

Parents' responsiveness to address their child's lack of progress increased because of timely notifications from teachers.[8] However, parents become even more keen than ever before to monitor their child's progress resulting in an increase in helicopter parenting. How does this impact the parent-child relationship? How does it impact their anxiety and stress? The constant surveillance puts students in a stressful environment where they may feel that their performance is always on display. What long term impact can this have on child development? These are important factors for teachers to take into consideration before implementing ClassDojo in their classrooms.

External factors such as parent engagement and family issues can significantly impact students' school performance. These factors are beyond a teacher's locus of control, and it is important for school administration to provide support that can help students negotiate the resulting daily tensions that may be beyond their ability to negotiate. Having guidance counselors available that students and parents can confide in without any repercussions can help them identify the challenges they are facing and come up with an action plan for students' performance at school.

What is the purpose of classroom management from an Islamic perspective?

Classroom management is not about achieving order for order's sake, but it is about achieving order so learning can occur. However, since character development is at the core of education in Islam, classroom management becomes one of the main approaches to *tarbiyah* and not just a means to establish a learning environment. This has important pedagogical implications on how to integrate ClassDojo, a CM tool, in our classrooms so they align with the purposes of CM for Muslim education.

Classroom management has three distinct purposes for Muslims:

1. Establish a safe learning environment for all.
2. Enhance student's physical, socio-emotional, intellectual, and spiritual growth.
3. Promote character development aligned with Islamic principles (*tarbiyah*).

Most of the first two purposes are commonly identified in CM literature.**Error! Bookmark not defined.** However, our understanding of the impact of CM on character development is still developing and Muslim teachers must approach the integration of any CM tool, such as ClassDojo, with great discretion.

ClassDojo's approach to managing student behavior through a token economy removes the focus on the higher *tarbiyah* goals intended for CM and reduces it to a set of individual points. CM should focus on character development, leadership, and motivating students through healthy relationships, inspiration (via role modeling), mutual respect, and team work to achieve common goals.

Some have cautioned educators on how ClassDojo achieves classroom compliance through discipline and intimidation.[43] They do not view the establishment of such an environment as necessarily conducive to a positive learning environment. Even the word "Dojo", a Japanese word for a place where people train in disciplined practice, indicates an outdated pedagogical paradigm where discipline and order are valued over other pedagogical approaches such as play and planned chaos.[2, 43] Muslim educators must carefully consider the trade we are making when we decide to implement ClassDojo in our classroom. What are we gaining and what are we losing in this exchange and how does that enable me to meet the goals of education in Islam?

Proactive Classroom Management Strategies

There are many proactive classroom management strategies that teachers can apply along with ClassDojo to maintain a positive learning environment for all. Here are some:

Engaging in meaningful activities

Engaging students through interactive learning activities will keep students busy with learning. Engaged students are less disruptive and contribute significantly to the overall learning environment. Focusing on meaningful student engagement is a proactive approach to teaching and will reduce the need to implement persuasive technologies such as ClassDojo. The ability to plan engaging lessons is one of the foundational skills for a teacher to have.

Best practices

A focus on research driven best practices allows for continuous improvement in teaching and learning. There are several tried and tested approaches to motivating students that teachers should implement with discretion:

- **Positive Behavior Intervention Supports (PBIS):** PBIS is a multi-tiered, praise-based intervention approach that supports the development of the whole child.[10] Informed by the field of applied behavior analysis, it uses proactive strategies to define, teach, and support actions that contribute towards a positive school culture. It uses the RTI approach (response to intervention) for early identification and support of students with learning and behavior concerns.[10] One of the strategies often used in PBIS is a token economy. Lately this has been facilitated by ClassDojo.[61] PBIS has been successfully adopted in many schools worldwide. Such universal strategies deserve more attention from educators in solving school problems. However, it is an approach to CM that has been developed within a secular framework. Therefore, Muslim educators should adopt it while making sure the implementation is aligned with the values and goals within the Islamic worldview.

- **Good Behavior Game (GBG):** In GBG students are divided into teams in their classroom, expectations are communicated clearly, teams are awarded points or lose points depending on their compliance with those expectations, and reinforcement is provided to those teams that earn points below a certain predetermined criteria.[60] Implementation of the GBG has been found to decrease disruptive behavior, increase academic engagement and productivity, decrease in concentration problems, and an increase in prosocial behavior mostly at the elementary school level.[65] Longitudinal studies of the cohorts that participated in GBG indicated reduction in substance abuse disorders, delinquency, incarceration, and suicidal ideation.[66] The positive reinforcement version of the GBG aligns with the Positive Behavior and Intervention Supports model of the positive psychology movement. It has been successfully facilitated using ClassDojo with increase in academically engaged behavior and decreases in disruptive behavior.[67]

- **Tootling:** A combination of the word "tattling" and "tooting your own horn," tootling is a classwide intervention developed by Skinner where students report on their peer's prosocial behaviors.[67] Students catch each other in the act of a prosocial behavior such as opening doors, giving verbal praise to each other, helping others, sharing, etc. and report it by writing it on a card and submitting it to the teacher. Though time consuming, tootling has demonstrated to effectively reduce disruptive behavior in elementary classrooms. Teachers have successfully used ClassDojo to overcome the time consuming aspect of tootling by having students report prosocial behaviors on ClassDojo.[4, 10, 60]

It is not just ClassDojo but a combination of best practices along with ClassDojo that results in positive outcomes for any interventions. Additionally, the strategies highlighted above must be implemented after careful consideration of their alignment with the Islamic worldview since they were developed within secular frameworks and may have unintended consequences that may be at odds with the goals of *tarbiyah*. Meaningful integration of ClassDojo with Best Practices (research driven) that are Islamically aligned can lead to effective classroom intervention strategies.

Relationship building

Teachers must be very intentional about forging strong student-teacher and student-student relationships. Integrating play, games, and team building activities will greatly facilitate the establishment of such relationships. Teacher praise, games like the Caterpillar Game or the Good Behavior Game can contribute significantly to a positive learning environment.[10] Strong relationships directly correlate with student cooperation and positive student-teacher relationships are more impactful in reducing problem behaviors than any other intervention.**Error! Bookmark not defined.**

Prophet Muhammad ﷺ paid great attention to fostering strong, positive connections with others. He ﷺ did this through honesty and integrity, humility and modesty, kindness and compassion, empathy and active listening, forgiveness and tolerance, by promoting justice and equality, by respecting diversity, and by encouraging cooperation and mutual support. He ﷺ did this not just with his ﷺ words but through his actions. He ﷺ led by example, consistently demonstrating the behavior and the values he preached. It is the mandate of every Muslim educator to follow this methodology of our beloved Prophet ﷺ.

Collaborative creation of class rules

Creating class rules collaboratively with students provides a sense of ownership and belonging in the classroom. This is critical to student well-being and development.[10] Centralizing the process of *shura* (mutual consultation) in decisions that significantly impact students will not only bring a sense of ownership but will also enable us to put our trust in Allah ﷻ and turn our classroom management into a meritorious act of *'ibadah*!

Allah ﷻ while talking about those who put their trust in Him ﷻ, highlights one of their actions as consulting with each other on important matters:

$$وَٱلَّذِينَ ٱسۡتَجَابُواْ لِرَبِّهِمۡ وَأَقَامُواْ ٱلصَّلَوٰةَ وَأَمۡرُهُمۡ شُورَىٰ بَيۡنَهُمۡ وَمِمَّا رَزَقۡنَٰهُمۡ يُنفِقُونَ (٣٨)$$

And those who respond to their Lord, and pray regularly, and conduct their affairs by mutual consultation, and give of what We have provided them. (Qur'an 42:38).

Moreover, Allah ﷻ commanded the Prophet ﷺ to consult with his ﷺ companions on matters that impacted them and once a decision has been made to put his ﷺ trust in Allah ﷻ:

$$فَبِمَا رَحۡمَةٖ مِّنَ ٱللَّهِ لِنتَ لَهُمۡ وَلَوۡ كُنتَ فَظًّا غَلِيظَ ٱلۡقَلۡبِ لَٱنفَضُّواْ مِنۡ حَوۡلِكَ فَٱعۡفُ عَنۡهُمۡ وَٱسۡتَغۡفِرۡ لَهُمۡ وَشَاوِرۡهُمۡ فِي ٱلۡأَمۡرِ فَإِذَا عَزَمۡتَ فَتَوَكَّلۡ عَلَى ٱللَّهِ إِنَّ ٱللَّهَ يُحِبُّ ٱلۡمُتَوَكِّلِينَ$$

$$(١٥٩)$$

It is by the grace from Allah that you were gentle with them. Had you been harsh, hardhearted, they would have dispersed from around you. So pardon them, and ask forgiveness for them, and consult them in the conduct of affairs. And when you make a decision, put your trust in Allah; Allah loves the trusting. (Quran 3:159).

When we consult with our students based on mutual respect, shared wisdom, and consideration of various perspectives, it fosters critical thinking, responsibility and accountability, patience, acceptance of Allah's ﷻ decree, and blessings from Allah ﷻ. It trains our students in the process of collective decision making, shared responsibility, and putting our trust in Allah ﷻ collectively.

Modeling, coaching, repetition and feedback

Students' social and emotional learning is often neglected in most schools and is not viewed as a factor contributing to students' success.[68] It is important for us to pay attention to students' SEL as it has a significant impact on students' success. Students lacking behavioral and social skills benefited from behavioral instruction that included modeling, coaching, repetition, and feedback.[69] This is the methodology of our beloved Prophet Muhammad ﷺ. Allah ﷻ refers to the Prophet ﷺ as the best example for everyone to follow (see Quran 33:21). The Prophet's ﷺ companions would imitate him ﷺ in all aspects of their life. Many were illiterate; therefore, modeling and learning by imitation served as the primary means of initial learning for many. Below are some approaches that leverage modeling, coaching, repetition, and feedback that are effective in guiding students to desirable behaviors.

Behavior analytic approach

Teachers can effectively guide students when they make informed decisions about classroom management and instructional approaches after identifying the skill deficits and overt problem behaviors in the classroom.[70] ClassDojo can provide some of the data points but not all. Other sources of data must come from classroom observers, conversations, interactions with students, students learning skills and work habits, meetings with parents, student surveys, etc. Teachers can then make sure their instructional strategies and guidance are responsive to the needs of the students. Such a comprehensive approach will capture some of the complexity of the classroom environment and will allow teachers to coach students targeting their holistic development.

Setting clear expectations

Students are motivated to meet expectations, follow rules, and complete schoolwork when teachers set clear expectations. Teachers should set attainable expectations to motivate students. When students are having difficulty meeting expectations then teachers should modify them to ensure expectations are within the zone of proximal development (ZPD). Timely feedback should be provided to students so they can adjust their efforts to meet expectations.

School wide culture

Classrooms must not operate in silos. They are part of a school wide system and all aspects of a classroom including the classroom management plan must be situated within this system. As such, there should be a clear school wide approach to classroom management that is driven by the Islamic framework for tarbiyah and is guided by the mission and vision of the school.

Policy documents such as the student code of conduct, school wide procedures, learning skills and work habits for students, student awards and recognitions, teacher/staff code of conduct, teacher/staff performance appraisals, etc. must be part of the guidelines that inform the development of a classroom management plan. Likewise, there should be a school wide student reward system in place to motivate students at the school wide level and to facilitate their positive behavior in the classroom.

All these elements contribute to a school wide culture with common understandings and ways of doing things and overcoming challenges (the PBIS approach highlighted above is one way to establish such a culture). ClassDojo, with its many school wide features, can greatly facilitate the establishment of a school wide culture. However, this culture should be carefully curated, established, and maintained while negotiating the many unintended consequences of integrating ClassDojo. All the above proactive strategies highlight the fact that ClassDojo should not be used in isolation and that it is just a minuscule part, only one of the many tools and approaches towards establishing a safe learning environment for all.

Impact on Student Motivation

It is very important that we examine the implementation of ClassDojo from the lens of motivating students. Teachers often do not consider all the different ways we can and should be integrating motivational elements in the classroom. A token economy is just one of the ways. Also, student motivation is based on a variety of factors, their likes/dislikes, preferences, previous experience, ability level, relationship between the teacher and student, how high stakes the class is, etc.

Teachers have associated the points and gaming feature of ClassDojo with increased student motivation and engagement.[10] The immediate feedback that students receive is similar to what has been identified as the Nintendo effect where player motivation and engagement is kept alive through immediate and continuous feedback.[71] This immediacy has also been identified as promoting self-regulation in students. Games also provide students control over the material by allowing them to learn at their own pace and by keeping it low stakes with do overs. All these gamification elements have shown to increase intrinsic motivation in students.[23] Therefore, it is not surprising that teachers have welcomed ClassDojo into their classroom as it brings in some of these elements of gamification. The challenge for educators though is to make sure that the "game" does not become the goal instead of a means to achieving a much larger goal, i.e. learning and character development.

Teachers have noted that most students lack intrinsic motivation and require tangible rewards to perform.[10] There is a concern that we are creating a generation that requires rewards for doing what is expected of them. Educators worry that extrinsically motivated students may not become life-long learners since that requires intrinsic motivation.[4] A personalized approach that blends both intrinsic and extrinsic motivational factors is likely to enhance student engagement in any curriculum setting.[23] Educators in the primary grades know that we have to start with extrinsic motivation with young children and gradually guide them towards intrinsic motivation.[21] Additionally, rewards have been shown not to decrease intrinsic motivation whereas verbal praise has been shown to increase it.[2] All of this alludes to the fact that motivating students is a highly complex and dynamic activity that should not be reduced to the use of a single tool or approach. Teachers should always be on the lookout for ways to motivate their students and exercise *hikmah* (wisdom) in guiding them.

Negative points or taking away points from students may demotivate them. Additionally, publicly displaying points in the classroom may demotivate students as they may lose face for losing points in front of their peers and teachers. Students expressed that they feel embarrassed, off task, far from the goal of getting the reward, angry, disappointed, and ashamed when teachers take away points, which can impact their performance and learning.[4]

Teachers may find it easier to rely on awarding and deducting points due to their immediate effect on student behavior. They may not take the extra step of providing verbal praise and feedback, which has been identified as the most incentivizing approach for motivating students. Verbal praise, the human connection, is important in forging teacher-student relationships that can inspire students.

Student engagement and motivation is multidimensional. Secular literature usually divides this multidimensional construct of motivation into three different types: behavioral, emotional, and cognitive.[23] There are several key secular theories on motivation that attempt to explain why people engage in certain behaviors and what drives them to pursue goals:

- **Maslow's Hierarchy of Needs:** Maslow organized human drive into a hierarchy, with basic physiological needs at the bottom and self-actualization at the top.[72] He posits that people fulfill their needs in a specific order, starting with the most basic needs of food, safety, and moving towards higher level needs of belonging, esteem, and self-actualization.

- **Self-Determination Theory (SDT):** Unpacks intrinsic and extrinsic motivation into three components, autonomy, competence, and relatedness.[73] People are most motivated when they feel in control of their actions, capable in their abilities, and connected to others.

- **Expectancy Theory:** People are motivated to act based on the belief that their efforts will lead to a desired outcome that will be valued.[74] *Expectancy*, the belief that effort will lead to a certain level of performance, *instrumentality*, the belief that performance will lead to a certain outcome, and *valence*, the value we place on the expected outcome, contribute to the level of motivation we have.

- **Goal Setting Theory:** Emphasizes the role of effective goals in increasing motivation.[75] Goals should be clear, measurable, challenging yet achievable to enhance motivation.

- **Attribution Theory:** Explains our motivation in terms of how we explain the causes of our successes and failures.[76] Our motivation is influenced by whether we attribute our outcomes to internal factors (ability, effort, etc.) or external factors (luck, task difficulty, etc.). Attributing our successes and failures to factors that are within the locus of our control increases motivation and resilience.

- **Self-Efficacy Theory:** Motivation is driven by our belief in our ability to succeed in a given task, i.e. our self-efficacy.[77] Self-efficacy can be nurtured by providing opportunities for success in "safe" environments, offering positive feedback, and by setting appropriate challenges.

- **Drive Theory:** Deconstructs motivation in terms of our need to fulfill biological drives such as hunger, thirst, etc.[78] These drives create tensions that motivate us to act with the goal of reducing these tensions.

- **Reinforcement Theory:** Highlights how behavior is reinforced through rewards and punishments.[79] Positive and negative reinforcement encourage behaviors, while punishment discourages them.

These theories dominate the contemporary psyche and understanding of human motivation. We can see elements of all or some of them in various programs and schemes that entice people towards material success. They are humanistic in their outlook where human agency is given precedence over any other power or ability. They provide an incomplete or a skewed perspective on the concept of motivation in Islam where the Power of Allah ﷻ and the concept of the Hereafter are centralized in effectuating change and in building our drive towards self-actualization.

Muslims need to approach these secular theories on motivation with a critical lens as they can easily misguide us in directions that are at odds with the purpose of life in Islam. Let's deconstruct one of these theories, Maslow's Hierarchy of Needs, to illustrate how it aligns with the concept of motivation in the Qur'an. Maslow says all of us have needs that we fulfill in a specific order, starting with the most basic needs and then moving up to more complex needs in our drive to seek happiness. These needs are typically represented as a pyramid (see Figure 1).

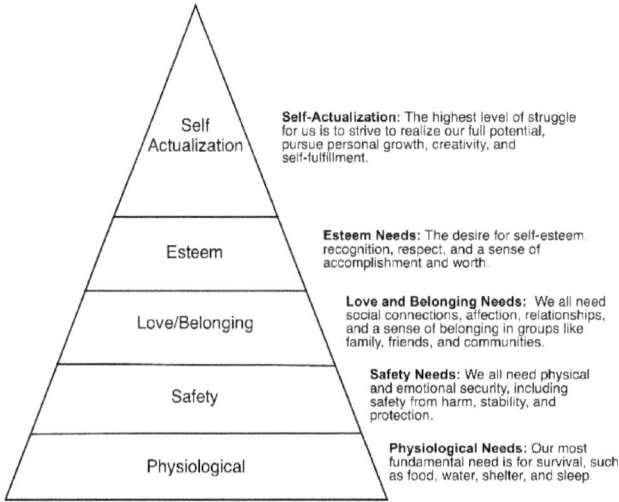

Figure 1: Maslow's Hierarchy of Needs

According to Maslow, in our drive for happiness and self-actualization/self-fulfillment, we must first satisfy lower-level needs (physiological and safety) before we can focus on higher-level needs (love/belonging and esteem).

In the Qur'an, Allah ﷻ directs our attention towards establishing a strong relationship with Allah ﷻ as the first step on our road to happiness and self-actualization. The other needs, though important, are not seen as a pre-requisite to attaining self-actualization. Rather they are made easier to attain for those who have a strong relationship with Allah ﷻ. We see this in the du'a of Ibrahim ﷺ that he makes upon leaving his family in the desolate valley of Makkah:

$$
رَبَّنَا إِنِّي أَسْكَنتُ مِن ذُرِّيَّتِي بِوَادٍ غَيْرِ ذِي زَرْعٍ عِندَ بَيْتِكَ الْمُحَرَّمِ رَبَّنَا لِيُقِيمُوا الصَّلَاةَ فَاجْعَلْ أَفْئِدَةً مِّنَ النَّاسِ تَهْوِي إِلَيْهِمْ وَارْزُقْهُم مِّنَ الثَّمَرَاتِ لَعَلَّهُمْ يَشْكُرُونَ
$$

Our Lord! I have settled part of my descendants in a barren valley, by Your sacred House, our Lord, that they may maintain the prayer. So make the hearts of a part of the people fond of them, and provide them with fruits, so that they may give thanks. (Quran 14:37).

Ibrahim ﷺ turns Maslow's pyramid of needs upside down! We would expect him to ask for the basic needs, food, water, and shelter first and then ask for safety and social needs for his family, but he starts with the establishment of prayer before asking Allah to fulfill their social needs then their basic needs, in that order. And he even connects these basic needs as means to connect with Allah ﷻ. This goes back to his other saying that Allah ﷻ captures for us in the Qur'an:

$$
قُلْ إِنَّ صَلَاتِي وَنُسُكِي وَمَحْيَايَ وَمَمَاتِي لِلَّهِ رَبِّ الْعَالَمِينَ (١٦٢)
$$

Say, "My prayer and my worship, and my life and my death, are devoted to Allah, the Lord of the Worlds. (Quran 6:162).

Allah ﷻ teaches us through Ibrahim ﷺ that striving for food, safety, and social needs should not become our primary targets in life for it is Allah ﷻ who determines how much and in what manner each of us will have these. Our primary drive should be to establish a strong relationship with Allah ﷻ for this will guarantee the fulfillment of other needs by Allah ﷻ.

The above example illustrates how one of the most popular secular theories on motivation is at odds with some of the core values in the Qur'an. It is important for Muslim educators to unpack such theories with reference to the Qur'an so we can identify and mitigate the resulting gaps as we plan instruction to motivate our students to achieve their full potential.

Lack of motivation in students is not easily definable or traceable.[8] Many factors can influence student motivation, relationship with the teacher, their personality, background, etc. Most secular literature on student motivation identifies student-teacher relationship as one of the most important factors that influences student motivation. This is true but in Islam this is further enhanced by connecting this relationship with our relationship with Allah ﷻ. For it is Allah ﷻ who inclines the hearts of people towards each other as stated to us in the following hadith:

وعنه عن النبي، صلى الله عليه وسلم، قال: "إذا أحب الله العبد نادى جبريل: إن الله تعالى يحب فلانًا، فأحببه، فيحبه جبريل، فينادي في أهل السماء: إن الله يحب فلانًا، فأحبوه، فيحبه أهل السماء، ثم يوضع له القبول في الأرض" (متفق عليه).

وفي رواية لمسلم : قال رسول الله صلى الله عليه وسلم: "إن الله تعالى إذا أحب عبدًا دعا جبريل، فقال : إني أحب فلانًا فأحببه، فيحبه جبريل، ثم ينادي في السماء، فيقول: إن الله يحب فلانًا، فأحبوه فيحبه أهل السماء، ثم يوضع له القبول في الأرض، وإذا أبغض عبدًا دعا جبريل فيقول: إني أبغض فلانًا، فأبغضه، فيبغضه جبريل، ثم ينادي في أهل السماء، إن الله يبغض فلانًا، فأبغضوه، ثم توضع له البغضاء في الأرض".

Abu Hurairah ؓ reported: The Prophet ﷺ said, "When Allah loves a slave, calls out Jibril and says: 'I love so-and-so; so, love him'. Then Jibril loves him. After that he (Jibril) announces to the inhabitants of heavens that Allah loves so- and-so; so love him; and the inhabitants of the heavens (the angels) also love him and then make people on earth love him". (Al- Bukhari and Muslim).

Another narration of Muslim is that the Messenger of Allah ﷺ said: "When Allah loves a slave, He calls Jibril (Gabriel) and says: 'I love so-and-so; so love him.' And then Jibril loves him. Then he (Jibril) announces in the heavens saying: Allah loves so-and-so; so love him; then the inhabitants of the heavens (the angels) also love him; and then people on earth love him. And when Allah hates a slave, He calls Jibril and says: 'I hate so- and-so, so hate him.' Then Jibril also hates him. He (Jibril) then announces amongst the inhabitants of heavens: 'Verily, Allah hates so- and-so, so you also hate him.' Thus, they also start to hate him. Then he becomes the object of hatred on the earth also". (Muslim). In *Riyad as-Salihin 387*.[80]

When teachers connect their students with Allah ﷺ, it will intrinsically motivate them to a level that cannot be achieved by any other means!

When we see that our students are not engaged or motivated to perform in our classroom then we should survey our students to identify the barriers that are keeping them from being engaged and motivated. You can survey your students by selecting some questions from the Student Engagement Instrument in Table 3 adapted from Brown (2021)[23] and modified to align with the Islamic framework.

In the survey below, you will find that some questions like *tahara* and *wudu* may seem unrelated to student engagement and motivation; however, they are some of the most fundamental prerequisites to maintaining a purpose driven, energetic lifestyle. Take *tahara* for example. It has a direct impact on our motivation and self-esteem because it establishes a routine of cleanliness and personal care thereby boosting self-discipline, it promotes mental clarity through mindfulness and self-reflection, it is a way of honoring our body, it connects our physical cleanliness with mental well-being, and it connects us with a higher purpose in life by getting us ready to connect with Allah ﷺ. Doing such ritualistic acts may seem very mundane but they have a much deeper impact on our motivation and self-esteem than we realize.

Table 3: Student engagement instrument

#	Question	Disagree	Not Sure	Agree
1	School is important for reaching my future goals.			
2	I plan to go to college after I graduate high school.			
3	I try my best to pay attention during class.			
4	I struggle to pay attention in class after recess.			
5	I find it difficult to concentrate when other students are distracting me.			
6	I don't understand why I get the grades I do.			
7	I should sit still and quite in class in order to learn new things.			
8	The rules at my school/class are fair.			
9	When I have problems at my school, my teachers are ready to help me.			
10	I enjoy talking to the teachers at school.			
11	I enjoy talking to the students at school.			
12	I feel nervous when I am at school.			
13	My teachers want me to keep trying when things are tough at school.			
14	I like to help others.			
15	I think earning points for good behavior helps me to stay focused in class.			
16	I enjoy earning points that can be traded for rewards.			
17	I will learn better when teachers give me a reward.			
18	ClassDojo helps me to stay focused when it is important to learn.			
19	I learn better when teachers use a game in the lesson.			
20	My parents/guardians are there for me when I need them.			
21	If I don't do well in school, it's because I'm not smart.			
22	Other students like me the way I am.			
23	Adults at my school listen to students.			

#	Question	Disagree	Not Sure	Agree
24	Other students care about me.			
25	Students at my school are there for me when I need them.			
26	My parents want to know when something good happens at school.			
27	Others respect what I have to say.			
28	I have friends at school.			
29	I feel safe at school.			
30	I am hopeful about my future.			
31	I pray five times a day.			
32	I ask Allah to forgive me when I make a mistake.			
33	I seek other people's forgiveness when I make a mistake.			
34	I forgive others when others apologize after they've hurt me.			
35	I love Prophet Muhammad ﷺ and try to follow his sunnah.			
36	I make du'a when facing any difficulty.			
37	I ask Allah (swt) first when I need something.			
38	I recite the Qur'an daily.			
39	I try to understand what Allah (swt) is telling me in the Qur'an.			
40	I follow the tahara rules carefully when using the washroom.			
41	I do my wudu carefully to make sure I'm completing all the steps as perfectly as I can.			
42	I do my azkar after salah.			

Conclusion

In the secular model of education, classroom management is simply used to facilitate academic achievement. Therefore, it may make sense to use a tool like ClassDojo to make classroom management more efficient. However, in the Islamic model of education, classroom management becomes one of the main platforms through which we can achieve the *tarbiyah* of our students. Therefore, it must be carefully curated. Classroom management is a dynamic and complex process and the one-dimensional approach of ClassDojo is not sufficient to achieve the goals of *tarbiyah*. It can be one of the many tools in the teacher's toolbox but not the first one and should not be the only one.

Teacher should go over the many proactive classroom management strategies outlined in this chapter before they move to more reactive strategies that are employed in ClassDojo. Establishing a school wide culture of care and love that promotes a strong relationship with Allah ﷻ and centralizes the way of the Prophet ﷺ will promote character development and student achievement. In the next chapter we will explore how technology, particularly ClassDojo, is impacting character development and how Muslims can realign it with the purpose of education in Islam.

5

CHARACTER DEVELOPMENT IN THE DIGITAL ERA

T he founders of ClassDojo have explicitly described its purpose as promoting character development. They consider human behavior as habitual and predictable; therefore, manipulable. Often such manipulation occurs through mandatory curricula and activities that seek to transform beliefs, attitudes, and dispositions through psycho-compulsion (imposition of psychological rationale). The app builds on the work of US KIPP charter schools' (Knowledge is Power Program) character development program that is grounded in the positive psychology of Martin Seligman, James Heckman and his work on the power of building character early in life, Angela Duckworth's work on persistence and grit, and Carol Dweck's work on the growth mindset.[5]

ClassDojo's categories of positive behavior are derived from KIPP school's seven character strengths necessary for leading an engaged, happy, and successful life: zest, grit, optimism, self-control, gratitude, social intelligence, and curiosity.[12] At first glance, these character traits may seem aligned with the goals of character development in Islam. However, a critical look at the purpose and the goal behind the app reveals several agendas that are driving the focus on character development.

KIPP schools have been criticized as a form of cultural sterilization and corporate cultural reform where human beings are viewed as a resource to be leveraged to maximize economic growth.[81] Any cultural values deemed as counterproductive to this goal are considered undesirable. ClassDojo heavily builds on this vision of character development where students are trained to take responsibility for the improvement of any shortcomings in their character through monitoring and labeling of student behavior. It is a more sophisticated and efficient expression of the factory model of education where the focus is on character development to maximize the human resource potential to increase corporate profit.

The Positive Psychology Movement and ClassDojo

ClassDojo gained popularity along with educational policies that were aligned with the positive psychology movement, the promotion of the growth mindset, and the increased interest in socio-emotional learning.[2] The psychological sciences have attempted for a long time to make visible the inner workings of a child's mind through scales, charts and other visual displays framed in norms of posture, habits, personality, and forms of conduct.[5] These scientific and technical imaginations of the child have transformed the child into an "object-child" reduced into manipulable, codable, mathematized two-dimensional calculations.[82] ClassDojo is a significant expression of this effort to "surveil, codify, calculate, predict and maximize the mental and emotional functioning of the child through normative classifications."[83]

Digital technologies shaping character

The World Economic Forum, in its 2016 article titled "New Visions for Education: Fostering Social and Emotional Learning Through Technology" has highlighted the potential of digital technologies in shaping students' character and developing their social and emotional proficiency to prepare them for a swiftly evolving digital economy.[84] Student data collected from technologies such as ClassDojo is being used to help policy makers and practitioners to better assess students' current skill sets and to identify future needs. This is informing the development of programs to help teachers and parents adapt their approaches to teaching and parenting and to adjust their learning and social environments accordingly.

It is important to prepare children for 21st century jobs. However, efforts in this regard are focused more on increasing human productivity with the intent of increasing economic efficiency. Significant and complex moral and ethical tensions arise due to the cultural diversity, given the global scale of these efforts. Instead of attempting to address these tensions, most of these efforts ignore them or silently background them for the focus is primarily on increasing economic productivity. Enamored by the promise of economic prosperity, many Muslim majority countries and Muslim individuals are adopting new technologies without giving serious consideration to their impact on character development and the Muslim identity.

Growth Mindset Promoted via ClassDojo

Growth mindset is part of the positive psychology movement promoted by PERTS and has been extended to business management focusing on the skills and talents of entrepreneurship in order to increase their ability to deal with challenges and risks and to learn from their mistakes.[5] The animated videos collaboratively produced by ClassDojo and PERTS advocate the use of the platform to promote growth mindsets in students. The platform is an expression on the global scale of the collaboration between the government and Silicon Valley venture investments that integrates new psychological and neuroscientific concepts with persuasive technologies to surveil children to modify their behavior to predetermined norms.

In addition to the materialistic intent behind the ClassDojo app, the issue with growth mindset is that it is implemented within a secularist ideology wherein values and what is right and wrong is dependent on the whims of the people and is continuously changing. In such a paradigm, growth mindset is a type of "open mindedness" where anything flies wherein "the end justify the means." Being rooted in a particular ideology is understood to be part of the fixed mindset, a negative mindset that is discouraged. This is problematic for Muslims as we are expected to be deeply rooted in Islamic values.

The Divinely endowed disposition towards good

Critics of growth mindset say that it reflects a deficit view of childhood where children, by default, are seen as incomplete.[41] In this sense, childhood is seen as something that needs to be improved upon until the child reaches an idealized state of adulthood. This doesn't align entirely with the Islamic view of the human being where every individual is endowed by Allah ﷻ with a sense of right and wrong:

ﻭَﻧَﻔْﺲٍ ﻭَﻣَﺎ ﺳَﻮَّﺍﻫَﺎ (٧) ﻓَﺄَﻟْﻬَﻤَﻬَﺎ ﻓُﺠُﻮﺭَﻫَﺎ ﻭَﺗَﻘْﻮَﺍﻫَﺎ (٨)

And the soul and He who proportioned it. And inspired it with its wickedness and its righteousness. (Quran 91:7-8).

Proportioning refers to the physical stature of the human being and the appropriate way to live in this world. Allah ﷻ has blessed us with the senses of sight, hearing, touch, taste, and smell through which we can learn. Allah ﷻ has endowed us with faculties of thinking, reasoning, imagination, memory, discrimination, judgement, will-power and other mental faculties by virtue of which we are able to use our senses effectively.

In addition, proportioning also means that Allah ﷻ has not created us as sinners by birth and as criminals by instinct. Instead, from the time of our birth, we are on the right and sound nature free from any inborn crookedness and are inclined to adopt the right path when we perceive it. Additionally, Allah ﷻ has endowed us with the faculty to discern right from wrong. Each one of us has a reproaching self (conscience) which reproaches us when we commit a wrong. In Islam children are expected to assume responsibilities as an adult gradually but at clearly defined times in their life (puberty, etc.). It is an obligation of parents and educators to prepare them for these responsibilities by nurturing and developing their God-given abilities.

Another critique of the growth mindset is that its focus on effort obscures the structural inequities that place marginalized students at a disadvantage.[41] Certain abilities, interests, and experiences that facilitate certain kinds of learning are prioritized over others. In most cases this is dictated by the values of the majority culture.

Some view ClassDojo's emphasis on growth mindset as misguided and overly focused on "fixing" the child. There may be other factors such as pedagogy, curriculum implementation, authenticity and validity of assessments, etc. that may significantly impact student achievement. Therefore, it is important for reflective practitioners not to rely too much on one tool or approach to closing the academic achievement gap. Rather, they should examine all factors that may contribute to achieving that goal.

Formation and curation of children's digital identity via ClassDojo

In ClassDojo, children are digital subjects whose identities are assessed through various metrics, such as likes and points, like those found on modern social media platforms. Rather than actively engaging with the application, students often become passive participants, being used by the system instead.[4] They become visible and measurable, while the underlying power dynamics remain hidden.[2] This allows children to focus on the task at hand and their results thereby becoming manageable within this specified framework. The close scrutiny of their behaviors heightens behaviorist disciplinary measures.[85] The use of reconstructed numerical data, such as ClassDojo points, supports data-driven governance techniques that rely on classifying, ranking, and comparing students. This de-contextualized representation of students' progress can potentially alter how they perceive their own identity and abilities.

Children may start viewing their self-worth in terms of their behavior points in ClassDojo. They may compare their points and rankings with peers, making them feel inadequate and competitive. This can have a detrimental impact on their self-esteem and how they relate with each other. Reducing children's performance to points can lead to fixed identities where children see themselves as either "good" or "bad". This can have a serious impact on their sense of agency where they may not see other possibilities for growth and development.

The role of *tawbah* in character development

The concept of *taubah* (repentance) in Islam plays a central role in the development of character. It teaches us to hold ourselves accountable for our actions and to find ways to redeem ourselves. It provides us with many possibilities for growth and development where mistakes are viewed as opportunities for improvement rather than failures. We are allowed to seek forgiveness from Allah ﷻ and are granted forgiveness by Him ﷻ through sincere repentance. The concept of *taubah* teaches us to empathize with others as we are taught that we must forgive others if we are to be forgiven by Allah ﷻ. Many of these dimensions of *taubah* may be lost when we operationalize character development via ClassDojo points.

Individual versus collaborative approach to character development

ClassDojo emphasizes individual improvement over the role of parents and other members of the community in shaping the education and character development of the child. The allure of the point system is a powerful stimulus to redirect children towards the targeted behaviors. It is problematic if those targeted behaviors are not aligned with the students' family values.

It does take a village to raise a child. But that can only happen when the values of various individuals in the village are aligned with each other. For Muslims, this alignment must be with the Qur'an and the sunnah. Parents have a very important role to play in the upbringing of children and teaching them right from wrong.

فَإِنَّ أَبَا هُرَيْرَةَ قَالَ قَالَ النَّبِيُّ صَلَّى اللَّهُ عَلَيْهِ وَسَلَّمَ مَا مِنْ مَوْلُودٍ إِلَّا يُولَدُ عَلَى الْفِطْرَةِ فَأَبَوَاهُ

يُهَوِّدَانِهِ أَوْ يُنَصِّرَانِهِ أَوْ يُمَجِّسَانِهِ كَمَا تُنْتَجُ الْبَهِيمَةُ بَهِيمَةً جَمْعَاءَ هَلْ تُحِسُّونَ فِيهَا مِنْ جَدْعَاءَ

ثُمَّ يَقُولُ أَبُو هُرَيْرَةَ رَضِيَ اللَّهُ عَنْهُ فِطْرَةَ اللَّهِ الَّتِي فَطَرَ النَّاسَ عَلَيْهَا

Abu Huraira ﷺ reported: The Prophet ﷺ said, "No child is born but that he is upon the natural instinct. His parents make him a Jew, or a Christian, or Magian. As an animal delivers a child with limbs intact, do you detect any flaws?" Then, Abu Huraira recited the verse, "The nature of Allah upon which he has set people," (Qur'an 30:30).[86]

Most children form their worldview between 15 to 18 months of age, and it is completely formed by the time they are 13 years old.[87] This worldview is unlikely to change until and unless there is a life changing crisis in the child's life. As the Prophet ﷺ indicated in the above *hadith*, parents play a crucial role in shaping the worldview of their children.

Many parents do not consciously nurture their children's worldview. This becomes problematic when children grow up in a majority culture that is not aligned with the Islamic worldview. This forces children to continuously negotiate the cross-cultural tensions that arise because of living in a majority culture that is different than their own. And this is further exacerbated when that majority culture is hostile to the Muslim identity.

Constantly negotiating the tensions between the Islamic worldview and the dominant secular worldview forces many children to adopt syncretism, a disparate, irreconcilable collection of beliefs and behaviors that is rooted in practical ethics.[88] It is a cut-and-paste approach to making sense and responding to life circumstances. It doesn't follow a consistent and coherent perspective on life. It is just based on what works, feels comfortable and convenient and often on what is popular. Muslim parents cannot afford to raise their children in such a haphazard manner. Parents should consciously commit to raising their children in an Islamic world view. Accordingly, there should be intentionality in all our interactions with our children, so we gradually shape their worldview in accordance with the Qur'an and sunnah.

Some may say that the points system feature in ClassDojo can also be leveraged to promote Islamic values. But even if the values are Islamic, it won't resolve the issue of sincerity of intentions behind our efforts as the points system will become the justification for all the students' actions. Our classroom expectations for students and their character development should be framed within the Islamic framework.

Islam's emphasis on character development

Islam places a lot of emphasis on character development. In fact, the Prophet ﷺ has said that people with the most complete faith are those with good character and will be closest to the Prophet ﷺ on the Day of Judgement:

عَنْ أَنَسٍ بْنِ مَالِكٍ أَنَّ رَسُولَ اللَّهِ صَلَّى اللَّهُ عَلَيْهِ وَسَلَّمَ قَالَ إِنَّ أَكْمَلَ النَّاسِ إِيمَانًا أَحْسَنُهُمْ خُلُقاً وإِنَّ حُسْنَ الْخُلُقِ لَيَبْلُغُ دَرَجَةَ الصَّوْمِ وَالصَّلَاةِ

Anas ibn Malik ﷺ reported: The Messenger of Allah ﷺ said, "Verily, the people with the most complete faith have the best character, for good character reaches the level of regular fasting and prayer." Reported in Musnad Al-Bazzar, Hadith 7445.[89]

عَنْ أَبِي هُرَيْرَةَ قَالَ قَالَ رَسُولُ اللَّهِ صَلَّى اللَّهُ عَلَيْهِ وَسَلَّمَ إِنَّ أَقْرَبَكُمْ مِنِّي مَنْزِلاً يَوْمَ القِيَامَةِ أَحَاسِنَكُمْ أَخْلَاقًا فِي الدُّنْيَا

Abu Huraira ﷺ reported: The Messenger of Allah ﷺ said, "Verily, those of you in the closest position to me on the Day of Resurrection are those of you with the best character in the world." Reported in Tarikh Dimashq, Hadith 6085.[90]

Understandably, character development has occupied center stage in the education of Muslim children historically as well as now. Given the character development focus of ClassDojo, can we leverage it to develop the character of Muslim children? If so, what adjustments need to be made to align it with the Islamic framework?

Character Development: Alignment in Purpose

In Islam, the ultimate goal of good character is to earn the pleasure of Allah ﷻ, which informs the altruistic spirit behind the doing of any good. Training students in purifying their intentions is a core concept in education in Islam. ClassDojo doesn't facilitate this very well and educators have highlighted this unintended consequence of ClassDojo's reward system.[2] ClassDojo's token economy system of immediate gratification through points and rewards is reductionist in nature and promotes self-centeredness through extrinsic motivation and is counterproductive to the spirit of altruism in Islam. Such an approach is out of sync with the concept of fitrah in Islam, the inborn God-given predisposition in each and every one of us that is inclined toward submission to Allah ﷻ through right action.

Purpose of education in Islam

The purpose of education is to nurture the God-given *fitrah* in us until we reach our full potential in complete submission to Allah ﷻ. This not only involves the further development of our fitrah but also protecting it from any corrupting environmental influences. Accordingly, establishing an Islamic environment in our classrooms is of paramount importance as children's fitrah is pure at birth.

An Islamic classroom environment connects children with Allah ﷻ by clearly articulating the purpose behind why we learn and why we strive to do good. Educators should carefully think about how ClassDojo can disrupt this purpose to deconstruct its corrupting influence. Here are some aspects to unpack with students:

- *Why do we do good?* Remind students daily about the importance of pleasing Allah ﷻ. Inspire them by telling stories that illustrate this important goal.

- *Shaytan's goal is to corrupt a person's good character.* Shaytan will try to make us commit the ultimate sin, shirk (associating partners with Allah ﷻ). If he fails in this then he will try to tempt us to disobey Allah ﷻ by committing acts forbidden by Allah ﷻ and by corrupting our character. Train students from a young age to seek refuge in Allah ﷻ from shaytan.

- *What makes us truly happy?* Unpack for students their feelings when they do good. Is it the extrinsic reward that makes them happy? Or is it pleasing the teacher and the parents that makes them happy? Or is it the class recognition that makes them happy? Or knowing that it pleases Allah ﷻ and He ﷻ would reward us for our goodness in the Hereafter that makes us happy? Can it be all of them as long as they align with earning the pleasure of Allah ﷻ? These questions help us to deeply connect with our fitrah.

- *Deconstruct for them the concept of temporary happiness and everlasting happiness.* This will help them to rationalize the sacrifices one must make to attain everlasting happiness.

- *Gradually wean children from extrinsic motivation to intrinsic motivation.* We live in a culture that thrives on the gratification of the self. Therefore, it is understandable for us to be influenced by this and more so for our children. Carefully plan out the rewards students receive through ClassDojo's token economy. Gradually minimize the extrinsic rewards as we move up the grade levels. Make the rewards less materialistic as you move up the grade levels.

Character Development: Alignment in Methodology

Allah ﷻ bears witness to the greatness of the Prophet's ﷺ character when He ﷻ says:

$$وَإِنَّكَ لَعَلَىٰ خُلُقٍ عَظِيمٍ$$

And you are of a great moral character. (Quran 68:4).

And Allah ﷻ tells us that we must follow the example of the Prophet ﷺ to attain the best character:

$$لَّقَدْ كَانَ لَكُمْ فِى رَسُولِ ٱللَّهِ أُسْوَةٌ حَسَنَةٌ لِّمَن كَانَ يَرْجُوا۟ ٱللَّهَ وَٱلْيَوْمَ ٱلْأَخِرَ وَذَكَرَ ٱللَّهَ$$

$$كَثِيرًا (٢١)$$

You have an excellent example in the Messenger of Allah ﷺ; for anyone who seeks Allah and the Last Day and remembers Allah frequently. (Quran 33:21).

Teachers must use the methodology of the Prophet ﷺ in developing the character of their students. The primary way that the Prophet ﷺ did this was by becoming a role model for others. ClassDojo backgrounds the importance of modeling good character because the focus is primarily on the students. Teachers must pay great attention to their own character and model it for their students. Here are some ways that we should consider foregrounding the teacher as a role model in the classroom:

- *Have the same expectations for yourself as you would for your students.* Explain to students that you also have the same commitment to follow classroom expectations. And model the classroom behaviors for the students. If we expect students to be polite then we must be polite with them as well. If we expect them not to yell at each other then we must also not yell at them. If we expect them to be considerate and not embarrass others, then we must do the same with our students.

- *Let your students know, like them, you too also struggled with meeting classroom expectations as a child and still struggle with maintaining good character all the time.* This will let students know that everyone struggles with maintaining good character. Let your students know that you make mistakes, but it is important to learn from one's mistakes.

- *Make it easy for students.* The Prophet ﷺ always opted for the easier option when following the rules of Allah ﷻ. So, make sure that you set realistic, age appropriate, and doable expectations for students.

- *Align and connect classroom expectations with the goals of tarbiyah in Islam.* Carefully think about what will be rewarded and what will be punished in the classroom. Make sure that it aligns with the Islamic expectations for character development.

- *Make astaghfar when not meeting classroom expectations.* Teach students to connect with Allah ﷻ immediately after they have disobeyed a rule or not met classroom expectations by having them say أَسْتَغْفِرُ ٱللَّٰه (*"astaghfirullah"*) to seek forgiveness from Allah ﷻ. This will train them from a young age that when they break rules, they are accountable to Allah ﷻ first before anyone else.

- *Always provide an opportunity for students to "redeem" themselves.* Centralize the concept of *taubah* in character development. Explain to students how even the best among us are prone to mistakes and how Allah ﷻ is always forgiving to those who want to return back to Him ﷻ.

ClassDojo is underpinned by a distinct political outlook and advocates a very specific brand of contemporary educational thought that "combines individualism, risk-taking, and the socially destabilizing potential of innovation.".[5] Powered by the Silicon Valley venture capitalism and governmentalization, ClassDojo's technocratic approach views education as a form of investment where children are products to be manipulated and shaped through behavior modification to achieve socio-economic ends. It tackles problems through more technological innovations that prefer efficiency rather than diving deeper into the anxieties that plague the depths of the human soul. The goal of education in Islam is to bring humanity out of the many darknesses that it is drowning into the Light of Allah ﷻ.

Being a Khalifah in a Digital World (Digital Citizenship)

Tarbiyah of young children must incorporate the Islamic principles of their role as *khalifah* in a digital world. Principles of digital citizenship, similar to those articulated by the International Society for Technology in Education should be incorporated in children's *tarbiyah* so they can become conscientious and critical producers and consumers of Big Data. The development and teaching of such an ethical conduct derived from Islamic beliefs will deter inappropriate digital activity.

Research on securing consumer data has primarily focused on the role of technology in cybersecurity and the mitigation and development of cybersecurity frameworks.[48] Little research, hence little insight, exists on the behavioral values that are needed to guide cyberspace interactions that would significantly enhance the security and privacy of consumer data. Islamic values and principles can play a big role in the ethical and moral development of Muslim children in the digitally driven world.

Ethical conduct in Islam is based on five principles:[48]

1. ***Tawheed:*** This is the central concept of monotheism and oneness in Islam. There is no god worthy of being worshipped except Allah ﷻ. From this comes a unified view of the world where Allah ﷻ is the source of all good; hence, all morals are derived from Him ﷻ.

2. **Justice and balance:** All ethical conduct must attempt to bring about justice and balance between various components and aspects of life to achieve harmony and equilibrium. This is one of the main functions in our role as khalifah of Allah ﷻ; caretaker of Allah's ﷻ creation.

3. **Freedom and free will:** Human beings have the freedom to choose, and that freedom must be maintained. However, it must be guided by a moral and ethical code of conduct derived from the Qur'an and from the sunnah of Prophet Muhammad ﷺ. This should also guide policies on online security and privacy.

4. ***Ihsan*** **or benevolence:** One of the highest forms of worship is to carry out beneficial actions for others without expecting anything in return. This should inform our online marketing policies and the exchange of user data in return for services.

5. **Responsibility and accountability:** All human beings are responsible for their actions and will be held accountable by

Allah ﷻ. We will be rewarded and punished in accordance with our actions.

These principles should always guide our conduct including in cyberspace.

Conclusion

Though ClassDojo has been targeted as a character development app, we have seen in this chapter that the intent behind the app doesn't align with the purpose of character development in Islam. It is informed by a secular worldview that is driven by materialistic goals. It is not aligned with the *fitrah* of the human being and doesn't follow the methodology of the Prophet ﷺ in character development.

The digital era presents unique challenges and opportunities, particularly for fostering character development in children. It is important for us to critically evaluate the many apps we use to complete daily tasks in the increasingly digitized world we live in and their impact on our character and digital identity. The themes on character development that we covered in relation to ClassDojo can also be extended to other apps. Our goal is to earn the pleasure of Allah ﷻ in everything that we do and to give priority to the Hereafter over this life. Creating a classroom environment that centralizes these core concepts of character development in Islam is essential in the development of the Muslim identity.

6

THE UNINTENDED CONSEQUENCES OF CLASSDOJO ON ISLAMIC VALUES AND THE MUSLIM IDENTITY

Postphenomenology suggests new technologies often promise revolutionary benefits but can also lead to unintended consequences. These unintended consequences occur because technology by design foregrounds (prioritizes and makes certain features or actions more prominent for ease of use) and/or amplifies certain ways of doing things while backgrounding (relegates other features to a less noticeable status) others. This influences how we interact with technology, what we focus on, and how different aspects of technology impact our daily lives.

In addition to the design choices made in the creation of technology, there are other factors that can lead to unintended consequences:

- **Incomplete understanding:** Technologies are developed under current/limited knowledge and understanding. When it is implemented in various contexts, new issues or effects may emerge that were unanticipated.

- **Short-term focus:** Technologies are often developed to solve immediate problems or to improve efficiency without fully considering the long-term implications. The pace at which new technologies are being developed and the temptation of leveraging it for economic gain further discourages designers from focusing on the long-term impact of technology.

- **Unpredictability of human behavior:** People use technologies in ways that designers may not foresee, which can lead to unintended consequences.

- **Scale and integration:** Technologies are initially developed to be used at a certain level and in specific circumstances but as the technology is scaled up and/or integrated in different aspects of life, it can lead to some unanticipated consequences.

Understanding and managing these unintended consequences requires ongoing research and a critical and reflective approach to using technology to foresee and mitigate any possible tensions that may arise due to the integration of technology in our lives. Let's take a deeper dive into how the use of ClassDojo in our classrooms can lead to some unintended consequences (UC) specially in regard to the Islamic values and the Muslim identity.

UC1: Inequity due to the digital divide

As with any technology, we must always ask who has access to the technology and how capable they are in using it effectively. The ClassDojo App can be downloaded on any smart device, making it accessible to all who have such devices and the supporting infrastructure (Internet access, etc.) to access all its features. However, not all parents may have access to the app. Additionally, I am aware of several parents that are unable to receive notifications from the app while at work because of the security restrictions at their workplace. This needs to be further researched to know how many parents do not have access or do not have continuous access to the app and to understand how this impacts their ability to participate in their child's education.

Do parents have enough digital literacy to use the ClassDojo app effectively? Not all parents have the same skill set when it comes to digital and media literacy.[10] What kinds of gaps does this create in parent participation? What kind of inequities does that create in terms of student achievement?

An important goal of education in Islam is to emancipate humanity from the allure of this materialistic world to the reality of life after death and to disconnect us from living a life without purpose to one that is guided by the Divine Light. Allah ﷻ reminds us of this purpose in the Qur'an:

اللَّهُ وَلِيُّ الَّذِينَ ءَامَنُوا يُخْرِجُهُم مِّنَ الظُّلُمَٰتِ إِلَى النُّورِ وَالَّذِينَ كَفَرُوٓا أَوْلِيَآؤُهُمُ الطَّٰغُوتُ يُخْرِجُونَهُم مِّنَ النُّورِ إِلَى الظُّلُمَٰتِ أُو۟لَٰٓئِكَ أَصْحَٰبُ النَّارِ هُمْ فِيهَا خَٰلِدُونَ (٢٥٧)

Allah is the Lord of those who believe; He brings them out of darkness and into light. As for those who disbelieve, their lords are the evil ones; they bring them out of light and into darkness—these are the inmates of the Fire, in which they will abide forever. (Qur'an 2:257).

Rabiah ibn 'Amir ﷺ highlighted this emancipatory mission of Islam when he responded to Rustam, the Commander-in-Chief of the Persian forces:

"Allah Azza wa jal has sent us to deliver you from worshiping the creation to worshiping the Creator of the creation and to deliver you from the constriction of this world to the vastness of this world and the hereafter and from the oppression of the religions to the justice of Islam. Allah Azza wa jal has sent us to save you from worshiping each other."[91]

Keeping this emancipatory mission of Islam, the Prophet ﷺ made sure that education remained accessible to one and all. We should be ever vigilant to make sure access to our educational systems doesn't unintentionally get limited by the technology we use and, in the process, creates inequities among students and within society.

UC2: Effects of digitally engineered classrooms

It is important to recognize the "artificially engineered" structure of contemporary classrooms and the challenges it poses to teachers. The contemporary elementary classrooms are crowded and more like a subway or bus than a place for learning. Students are expected to behave as if they are in solitude while in fact they are not! Studies have identified six features of the classroom that make it a complex place to manage:**Error! Bookmark not defined.**

1. **Multidimensionality:** classrooms are expected to be used for a broad range of activities and events (reading, writing, discussions, socialization, playing, instruction, counselling, meeting students/parents, etc.).
2. **Simultaneity:** Many activities occur simultaneously in different places in the same classroom. Sometimes we see this formally occurring via learning centres and at other times informally and discreetly occurring among students.

3. **Immediacy:** The combination of the many short periods-based school wide schedule and the quick pace at which lessons unfold make it difficult to think through every action ahead of time.

4. **Unpredictability:** It is difficult to anticipate how the day will unfold despite careful planning. Just the sheer number of students in a classroom increases the unpredictability.

5. **Lack of privacy:** often events unfold in full display of everyone in the classroom.

6. **History:** Classrooms, like families remember past events, both positive and negative. Additionally, many structures in the classroom (both soft and hard) have been historically determined. Some of these structures are from an era past and may either facilitate or inhibit learning when they clash with new digitally informed structures.

It is because of these six elements commonly found across classrooms that teachers spend more time managing behavior as opposed to enabling students to learn. Effective teachers are those that can plan student centered engaging lessons that can maintain students' focus and motivation to learn despite these challenges.

ClassDojo has been designed to either facilitate or manage and in some cases take advantage of these six classroom features. ClassDojo's ability to keep track of student behaviour and to communicate that in real time enables teachers to adapt it to the multidimensionality, simultaneity, immediacy and unpredictability of the classroom environment. Teachers can provide immediate feedback on student behavior to students as well as to parents. Using technology to mediate between the teacher and the student puts a distance that can alienate them from each other. One must ask how does such engineering of our classrooms shape the way we teach and learn? What unintended consequences does it have?

Instead of using such technologies to maintain digitally engineered classrooms, we should think about changing the structure of the classroom itself so learning can become more intimate. Such intimacy is needed to foster the love and care between the teacher and the student so we can motivate and inspire students. Such structural changes require us to question the status quo and to think outside the box. Most Islamic schools in North America follow the curriculum from government agencies with addons like Islamic studies, Qur'an, and Arabic. Some go a bit further by trying to "Islamize" the secular curriculum through cross curricular integration of Islam. These schools are structured just like any other public school and follow the factory model of schooling. **We need to restructure our schools to facilitate the Qur'anic model of teaching and learning.**

UC3: Distancing from reality

Games and virtual environments create an alternate reality that can lead to skewed perspectives. The imaginary avatars in gaming, not unlike the monsters in ClassDojo, have the potential to distance players from reality.[7] Student Stories, a feature in ClassDojo where students can add their own account of classroom experiences by annotating pictures with voice recordings that are viewable by parents, may further distance students from their actual experiences if not monitored carefully by the teachers.[92] This can also create an echo chamber where parents may amplify their child's voice over that of the teacher's.

Virtual worlds offer safe environments in which students can safely learn from their mistakes. The virtual reality created by ClassDojo can have certain positive impacts such as:

1. **Provides a safe distance:** The Dojo monsters provide an imaginative and friendly way for children to explore classroom

behaviors. They can use the Class Story to create a story line in a protected environment where they can explore the impact of their behaviors on the monster from an emotionally "safe distance". This may allow them to better unpack their behaviors and to understand their impact on them, others, and the classroom environment.

2. **Enhanced engagement:** the monsters are attractive and child friendly, making compliance with classroom expectations immersive and more enjoyable.

3. **Exploration of complex themes:** Teachers can use the fictional and fantastical nature of the avatars in ClassDojo to discuss the impact of classroom behavior on the monster. This allows them to discuss with children complex social challenges that students encounter in a school environment.

At the same time, excessive self-identification with the ClassDojo monsters may distance children from reality and lead to skewed perspectives about the impact of their behavior, especially when it is reduced to the awarding and taking away of points. The Student Story feature can distract students from what is going on in the classroom and pay more attention to their own student story.

Islam places great emphasis in guiding children towards the right perspective regarding their lived experiences. Teachers are expected to teach their students the right perspective on faith and the importance of recognizing their responsibilities toward Allah ﷻ and the world. The Quran and hadith emphasize the importance of developing and maintaining good character and moral behavior. For example, the Prophet ﷺ in one of the *hadiths* says:

عَنِ ابْنِ عَبَّاسٍ قَالَ قَالَ رَسُولُ اللهِ صَلَّى اللهُ عَلَيْهِ وَسَلَّمَ خِيَارُكُمْ أَحَاسِنُكُمْ أَخْلَاقًا الْمُوَطَّؤُونَ أَكْنَافًا وَشِرَارُكُمُ الثَّرْثَارُونَ الْمُتَشَدِّقُونَ الْمُتَفَيْهِقُونَ

Ibn Abbas ﷺ reported: The Messenger of Allah ﷺ said, "The best of you are those with the most excellent character and are careful of those around them. The worst of you are the pompous, the braggarts, and the pretentious." Source: Shu'ab al-Imān lil-Bayhaqī 7621. Grade: Sahih (authentic) according to Al-Albani.[93]

We live in times where truth has become relative and keeping a non-judgmental attitude and an open mind regarding character and morals is seen as a virtue. There are many skewed perspectives on the importance of character and what is considered "good" character. It is our duty as educators to guide students towards the Islamic values on good character and morals and to help them see the connection between classroom behavior and character development. This is one of the core functions of education in Islam.

Teachers should take the time to unpack the impact of classroom behaviors on fellow classmates and the learning environment so students can gain a deeper understanding of the impact of their actions on others. Providing venues for students to reflect in class about their behavior should become part of the classroom culture. For example, having students write reflection sheets, reflection journals, thank you notes, etc. can help students understand the impact of their actions on others.

UC4: Centralization of School Culture

Now schools can sign up for ClassDojo accounts that allow teachers and school leaders to safely share photos, videos, messages, points on a school wide basis. Some have viewed this as the creep positioning of ClassDojo as a behavioral surveillance platform that extends beyond the classroom walls to the school principal's office and out to the students' homes.[5] ClassDojo is altering schools through the use of a centralized digital network and creating a culture where students are self-conscious of performing.[41]

ClassDojo is also seeking to integrate into some of the core administrative tasks such as communication with parents and staff. One of the promotional emails from ClassDojo highlights an example of a daily memo from Principal Lamb to encourage school leaders to use the messaging feature of the app to send daily memos to their teams.[94]

This centralization better positions people who are in control to amplify certain values and cultures over others. Muslim educators can use these features of ClassDojo to establish and maintain a schoolwide Islamic environment. Islamic school leaders should have a schoolwide communication plan that clearly articulates ClassDojo's role in this plan.

UC5: Decrease in F2F interactions

Students, more females than males, agreed that ClassDojo reduces the frequency of face-to-face (F2F) interviews with families and teachers.[8] A significant number of parents were concerned about the decline in F2F meetings with teachers. In the same study, students viewed the decrease in F2F interviews with parents due to ClassDojo as a positive outcome. Though the decrease in F2F interviews with parents due to ClassDojo use is seen as a positive outcome, an unintended consequence of this is that teachers' interactions with parents becomes more digital and less human. What implications does this have on the teacher-parent relationships?

It is problematic if teachers use ClassDojo as the primary means to deploy their classroom management plan because the tool then becomes the platform through which the teacher is interacting with students. What kind of relationship does this establish between the teacher and the student? Can teachers have a "heart to heart" connection with their students when their relationship is negotiated through such a technologically driven platform?

F2F interactions provide the human touch that is essential for showing care, connecting emotionally, and building trust. Whether it is a kind word, eye contact, body language, a pat on the back or a handshake, these physical interactions play a powerful role in establishing relationships that can motivate and inspire parents and students. There are many examples of the Prophet ﷺ that demonstrate how he ﷺ centralized physical touch and F2F interactions in redirecting and motivating his ﷺ students, the sahabah (may Allah be pleased with them).

The Prophet ﷺ used his gentle and compassionate touch to foster an environment of care, correction, and connection. He ﷺ would use his reassuring touch to guide his companions back to the right path. Here's one example:

عَنْ أَبِي أُمَامَةَ قَالَ إِنَّ فَتًى شَابًّا أَتَى النَّبِيَّ صَلَّى اللَّهُ عَلَيْهِ وَسَلَّمَ فَقَالَ يَا رَسُولَ اللَّهِ ائْذَنْ لِي بِالزِّنَا فَأَقْبَلَ الْقَوْمُ عَلَيْهِ فَزَجَرُوهُ قَالُوا مَهْ مَهْ فَقَالَ ادْنُهْ فَدَنَا مِنْهُ قَرِيبًا قَالَ فَجَلَسَ قَالَ أَتُحِبُّهُ لِأُمِّكَ قَالَ لَا وَاللَّهِ جَعَلَنِي اللَّهُ فِدَاءَكَ قَالَ وَلَا النَّاسُ يُحِبُّونَهُ لِأُمَّهَاتِهِمْ قَالَ أَفَتُحِبُّهُ لِابْنَتِكَ قَالَ لَا وَاللَّهِ يَا رَسُولَ اللَّهِ جَعَلَنِي اللَّهُ فِدَاءَكَ قَالَ وَلَا النَّاسُ يُحِبُّونَهُ لِبَنَاتِهِمْ قَالَ أَفَتُحِبُّهُ لِأُخْتِكَ قَالَ لَا وَاللَّهِ جَعَلَنِي اللَّهُ فِدَاءَكَ قَالَ وَلَا النَّاسُ يُحِبُّونَهُ لِأَخَوَاتِهِمْ قَالَ أَفَتُحِبُّهُ لِعَمَّتِكَ قَالَ لَا وَاللَّهِ جَعَلَنِي اللَّهُ فِدَاءَكَ قَالَ وَلَا النَّاسُ يُحِبُّونَهُ لِعَمَّاتِهِمْ قَالَ أَفَتُحِبُّهُ لِخَالَتِكَ قَالَ لَا وَاللَّهِ جَعَلَنِي اللَّهُ فِدَاءَكَ قَالَ وَلَا النَّاسُ يُحِبُّونَهُ لِخَالَاتِهِمْ فَوَضَعَ يَدَهُ عَلَيْهِ وَقَالَ اللَّهُمَّ اغْفِرْ ذَنْبَهُ وَطَهِّرْ قَلْبَهُ وَحَصِّنْ فَرْجَهُ فَلَمْ يَكُنْ بَعْدُ ذَلِكَ الْفَتَى يَلْتَفِتُ إِلَى شَيْءٍ

Abu Umamah ﷺ reported: A young man came to the Prophet, peace and blessings be upon him, and he said, "O Messenger of Allah, give me permission to commit adultery." The people turned to rebuke him, saying, "Quiet! Quiet!" The Prophet said, "Come here." The young man came close, and he told him to sit down. The Prophet said, "Would you like that for your mother?" The man said, "No, by Allah, may I be sacrificed for you." The Prophet said, "Neither would people like it for their mothers. Would you like that for your daughter?" The man said, "No, by Allah, may I be sacrificed for you." The Prophet said, "Neither would people like it for their daughters. Would you like that for your sister?" The man said, "No, by Allah, may I be sacrificed for you." The Prophet said, "Neither would people like it for their sisters. Would you like that for your aunts?" The man said, "No, by Allah, may I be sacrificed for you." The Prophet said, "Neither would people like it for their aunts." Then, the Prophet placed his hand on him, and he said, "O Allah, forgive his sins, purify his heart, and guard his chastity." After that, the young man never again inclined to anything sinful. Source: Musnad Aḥmad 22211. Grade: Sahih (authentic) according to Al-Arna'ut.[95]

Just imagine the above scene playing out and how the Prophet ﷺ is connecting with the young man by asking him to sit close to him, helping him to view the question from an empathetic perspective, and putting his hand on him and making du'a for him. We see this strategy of using physical proximity to connect deeply with others used again and again by the Prophet ﷺ. We may be willing to let go of F2F interactions out of the convenience technology may afford. We should not trivialize the importance of F2F interactions and the physical touch in connecting with others and redirecting them even if it means a bit of an inconvenience for us.

Many educators realize the importance of physical connection and F2F interactions. In one study, teachers intentionally chose not to communicate with parents regarding individual student matters via ClassDojo.[10] They preferred speaking to parents in person or over the phone regarding disruptive behavior, citing how written messages did not always convey what was intended to be communicated. Teachers preferred students to be present while speaking with parents as opposed to sending messages. These were some of the strategies teachers utilized to maintain in-person interactions with parents.

UC6: Compromises the empathetic approach to redirecting students

Studies have recommended teachers to give positive points and send positive messages to parents more frequently than negative ones as the negative points and messages demotivate students.[8] The "dings" that alert students when a point is awarded or taken remove the human touch while still putting student performance on display in front of the whole class. The care and compassion that a teacher can deliver while still redirecting or even reprimanding a student cannot be replicated by these inhuman dings!

Researchers have raised philosophical concerns regarding ClassDojo's long-term impact on teacher-student interactions and its pedagogy using behaviorist, gamified, and token economy approaches.[2] How empathetic can a teacher be when their interactions with students is mediated through ClassDojo? What impact does this technical awarding and deduction of points to redirect students have on the socio-emotional development of children? Can such a technical approach to dealing with children behavior nurture empathy in them? Will these children do the same when they interact with others by just focusing on the behavior correction without giving a second thought to the feelings of those whom they are correcting?

As described previously, Allah ﷻ describes Prophet Muhammad's ﷺ approach to dealing with others as one that was driven with mercy and compassion:

$$\text{لَقَدْ جَاءَكُمْ رَسُولٌ مِّنْ أَنفُسِكُمْ عَزِيزٌ عَلَيْهِ مَا عَنِتُّمْ حَرِيصٌ عَلَيْكُم بِالْمُؤْمِنِينَ رَءُوفٌ رَّحِيمٌ (١٢٨)}$$

There has come to you a messenger from among yourselves, concerned over your suffering, anxious over you. Towards the believers, he is compassionate and merciful.
(Quran 9:128).

What can teachers do to ensure they are not losing this dimension of mercy and compassion while using ClassDojo as a classroom management tool?

The Prophet ﷺ has used the analogy of the mirror to compare the relationship between believers:

عَنْ أَبِي هُرَيْرَةَ عَنِ النَّبِيّ صلى الله عليه وسلم قَالَ الْمُؤْمِنُ مَرْآةُ أَخِيهِ وَالْمُؤْمِنُ أَخُو الْمُؤْمِنِ يَكُفُّ عَلَيْهِ ضَيْعَتَهُ وَيَحُوطُهُ مِنْ وَرَائِهِ وقال أبو هريرة الْمُؤْمِنُ مَرْآةُ أَخِيهِ إِذَا رَأَى فِيهَا عَيْبًا أَصْلَحَهُ

Abu Huraira ؓ reported: The Prophet ﷺ said, "The believer is a mirror to his faithful brother. He protects him against loss and defends him behind his back." Abu Huraira said, "The believer is a mirror to his brother. If he sees something wrong in him, he should correct it." Source: al-Adab al-Mufrad 239[96]

Just like how a mirror offers a silent critique of the person looking into it, a Muslim is expected to redirect a fellow Muslim discreetly and gently without exposing them unnecessarily and without embarrassing them. ClassDojo blatantly puts student infractions in front of the whole class and indirectly teaches students to redirect others in a sterile and crude manner.

It is problematic if teachers use ClassDojo as the primary means to deploy their classroom management plan because the tool then becomes the platform through which the teacher is interacting with students. What kind of relationship does this establish between the teacher and the student? Can teachers have a "heart to heart" connection with their students when their relationship is negotiated through such a technologically driven platform?

UC7: Removes focus from learning to behavior management

The continuous evaluation of student behavior where everything is quantified removes students' focus from learning to behavior management. Teachers provide continuous feedback to students on their behavior by giving and taking away points. In many cases this is becoming the primary form of feedback in classrooms where teachers and students are prioritizing behavior over academic achievement.

Intellectual engagement plays a crucial role in reducing the need for extensive behavior management because when students are meaningfully engaged in the learning process, they are less likely to disengage or act out. Developing student centered lessons with hands on activities will make learning more meaningful for students. Integrating the daily challenges and concerns of students in lessons will make learning more relevant. These are some proactive approaches to teaching that teachers must give priority to instead of focusing on reactive approaches such as behavior management.

UC8: Gamification and Promotion of Competition

ClassDojo follows the trend in gamification of education where online platforms are increasingly being used to control student behavior through a point system.[4] Despite the value of educational games, many view their reliance on extrinsic motivation as short-term solutions where the primary focus is on becoming "winners". Such games motivate students to learn only when external rewards are provided. Such motivation diminishes with time and if not replaced with intrinsic motivation can have a detrimental impact on long-term academic success.

ClassDojo's gamified approach to behavior management makes it a persuasive, habit-forming technology where children's behavior is commodified. Children gain points through their behaviors that can be exchanged for rewards. Behaviors that are deemed appropriate to developing a growth mindset are rewarded. As such, some have called it a technology of psycho-compulsion and behavior modification.[4]

Games provide a safe space for students to make mistakes and practice their skills. However, one of the unintended consequences of gaming is that it disconnects us from our lived reality. ClassDojo's focus on points and rewards for expected behavior distorts the real purpose of "good" behavior and that is to please Allah ﷻ and to build and manage relationships. Students' may focus more on gaining points through their behavior rather than thinking about how their behaviour may have impacted others and how it impacts their relationship with Allah ﷻ. This element of empathy and relevance is backgrounded when behaviors are commodified into a point system.

ClassDojo gamifies behavior management in the classrooms and with its "ClassDojo Beyond School" paid component, this gamification seems to be extending to parenting as well. The public display of points encourages a competitive environment and shames students.[4, 41] A competitive environment creates stress and if not managed well can reinforce negative behaviors and negatively impact students' sense of belonging and participation.[4] Should children be motivated to behave well because that is what they are supposed to do or for rewards and to compete?

A gamified approach to managing behavior seemingly empowers the teacher while making the students passive learners. I say that it seemingly empowers the teachers because the teacher's role is dominated by the point system where the teacher's efficacy is compromised.[4, 23] The point system limits the teachers' vision and they are unable to monitor and unpack the different classroom interactions. This results in critical areas of the learning environment being neglected and leads to lost learning opportunities.[10]

Teachers are in a powerful position to influence the classroom environment and if they play their role responsibly as a *murabbih* then they can play a central role in shaping the character of their students. This requires teachers to forge relationships with their students where they connect with them at a very deep socio-emotional and intellectual level. It requires teachers to teach with a "heart", something that may be lost when the classroom environment is relegated to a point system.

UC9: Standardization of behaviors

ClassDojo promotes a specific set of behaviours derived from growth mindset from the positive psychology movement. Its animated video series that were viewed more than 15 million times within 6 months of being launched illustrate the rapid and global diffusion of new forms of psychological expertise that seeks to modify student behavior and practices in the classroom through constant monitoring, measuring, and manipulating.[5] It has led to the standardization of a particular sets of behaviors derived from very specific cultural values of Silicon Valley venture capitalism, venture labour, government agendas, and new sciences of psychology at the cost of sterilization of other cultures. I've dedicated an entire chapter on character development to unpack this in more details (see Chapter 5).

Since there is the possibility of standardization of behaviors, teachers must exercise high discretion in selecting the targeted behaviors. Additionally, teachers should be attuned to the cultural behavior norms so they can accommodate the differences in their classrooms. Perhaps targeting different behaviors on a monthly or bi-monthly basis can allow for greater diversity of student expression in the classroom. Teachers can also use the points feature to target various *sunnahs* of Prophet Muhammad ﷺ and train students in them.

UC10: Focus on personal improvement over structural problems

ClassDojo's prioritization of personal improvement over addressing structural issues by focusing on "technical fixes" and "solutionism" is part of the culture of Silicon Valley tech companies.[5] In this culture, psychological initiatives derived from behavioral economics are seen as ways of optimizing employee attitudes and behaviours. It is a technocratic ideology that attempts to solve all problems, including behavioral problems, through a combination of psychological research and technological development.

Standford University, located in the Silicon Valley, has applied these concepts to education with its:

- PERTS lab that explores the integration of growth mindset in education,
- Standford Lytics Lab that applies new data analytics techniques to the measurement of non-cognitive learning factors such as perseverance, grit, etc., and

- the Persuasive Technologies Lab that focuses on the development of machines designed to influence human beliefs and behaviors.

Such a technocratic approach is highly reductionist and trivializes the role of other factors such as the environment, socialization, emotional development, and spiritual motivation in shaping human behavior. More than anything else, it dismisses the role of Divine guidance (*hidayah*) in the development of the child.

Muslims should seek solutions to the challenges they face in a comprehensive manner. First and foremost, we must seek guidance from Allah ﷻ and put our *tawakkul* (trust) in Him ﷻ. We should exercise *hikmah* (wisdom) to understand the situation and act with insight to balance various factors. We should maximize the benefit and minimize the harm to all. When we do this, we will come up with comprehensive solutions that may not be perfect but will better align with Islamic values, fostering personal growth, harmony, and social responsibility.

UC11: Stigmatization of "undesirable" behavior

The public display of points stigmatizes any behaviors that teachers consider undesirable.[41] Students exhibiting such behaviors may be marginalized or their identity may be overshadowed with feelings of shame and regret. Stigmatization is characterized by dehumanization, exclusion, and lack of empathy. All these aspects can easily become prevalent via ClassDojo's point system. Therefore, it is important for teachers to be empathetic, understanding and supportive in addressing student behaviors to motivate them to overcome challenges.

Here are some strategies teachers can use to prevent stigmatization and promote a positive and understanding classroom culture:

- Set clear expectations.

- Focus on the behavior not the student.

- Use language that is non-judgmental.

- Be empathetic and provide a path to identify underlying causes.

- Focus on desirable behavior and model it for the students.

- Centralize the role of *tawbah* (repentance) as a restorative practice wherein students can reflect on their actions, understand the impact on themselves and others, and find a constructive path forward.

- Involve individuals from students' immediate circle of influence.

UC12: Fosters Perfectionism

The ability to report to parents in real-time fosters the development of perfectionism in children and puts undue stress on them.[41] Teachers have stated that it is much easier with ClassDojo to report student behavior to parents immediately and document it at the same time.[10] However, this doesn't allow students to "break the bad news" to the parents. The constant surveillance puts students in a stressful environment where they may feel that their performance is always on display. What long term impact can this have on child development? What kind of identity develops when students are trained from a very young age to be self-conscious of performing?

While striving for excellence and doing one's best is highly encouraged in Islam, the pursuit of perfection should not lead to feelings of inadequacy, frustration, or despair. Muslim children are taught from a young age the importance of *taqwa*, the state of mind that Allah ﷻ is always watching us and knows and sees what we do. We are taught the related concept of *Ihsan*, doing things as if we see Allah ﷻ and if we are unable to do that then to act as if He ﷻ sees us. *Ihsan* also means to do things with excellence to please Allah ﷻ. However, while doing so, we should not set unrealistically high standards and should not be excessively critical of ourselves as it can become counterproductive.

We must help students realize that perfectionism is not always attainable nor required. Our deeds are rewarded according to our intentions and the amount of effort we put. Our reward is preserved with Allah ﷻ regardless of the outcome. This understanding reduces the stress among students to perform with perfection. Allah ﷻ appreciates sincere striving and accepts our efforts as acts of worship and rewards us for them.

We should encourage students to practice *muhasaba* (self-reflection, self-accountability, and self-evaluation) so they can identify where they fell short regarding the standards and expectations and make *tawbah*, turn to Allah ﷻ with repentance and for guidance. Perfectionism often breeds self-criticism, which can make us feel distant from Allah's mercy. Allah's Mercy is greater than His anger and Allah loves to forgive. Sincere repentance erases any unintentional or intentional mistakes. Lastly, we must encourage students to practice *wasatiyyah* (moderation) in all aspects of life as this will help them avoid over-perfectionism. Only Allah ﷻ is perfect. Everyone else strives to do their best according to their abilities and available resources.

UC13: Promotes Adultism

Some view the depiction of children in ClassDojo as monster avatars as an expression of adultism; a form of systematic discrimination against young people where children are assumed to be less human than adults.[41] In this sense, ClassDojo distinguishes between the "human" teacher and her "monstrous" students. This may further reinforce the stereotype that children are not able to make decisions and may lead to a lack of consideration for children's personal choices and autonomy. This

146

underestimation of their abilities can have serious implications on providing them with opportunities for growth.

We find many examples in the Qur'an and in the life of Prophet Muhammad ﷺ that illustrate the importance of engaging children at a very high intellectual level and as active participants in decision making and in discourses that impact our lives. For example, we see in the Qur'an, Prophet Ibrahim عليه السلام consulting with his son, Ismail عليه السلام about his dream in which he saw himself sacrificing his son to Allah ﷻ:

فَلَمَّا بَلَغَ مَعَهُ ٱلسَّعْيَ قَالَ يَٰبُنَىَّ إِنِّىٓ أَرَىٰ فِى ٱلْمَنَامِ أَنِّىٓ أَذْبَحُكَ فَٱنظُرْ مَاذَا تَرَىٰ قَالَ يَٰٓأَبَتِ
ٱفْعَلْ مَا تُؤْمَرُ سَتَجِدُنِىٓ إِن شَآءَ ٱللَّهُ مِنَ ٱلصَّٰبِرِينَ (١٠٢)

Then, when he was old enough to accompany him, he said, "O My son, I see in a dream that I am sacrificing you; see what you think." He said, "O my Father, do as you are commanded; you will find me, Allah willing, one of the steadfast." (Quran 37:102).

Ibrahim عليه السلام knows that his dreams, as a prophet of Allah, are true visions, yet he still consults with his son and seeks his opinion. He actively engages him in this decision that is going to impact him with serious consequences.

The Prophet ﷺ is likewise ordered by Allah ﷻ to consult with his companions in decisions that impact them:

فَبِمَا رَحْمَةٍ مِّنَ ٱللَّهِ لِنتَ لَهُمْ وَلَوْ كُنتَ فَظًّا غَلِيظَ ٱلْقَلْبِ لَٱنفَضُّوا۟ مِنْ حَوْلِكَ فَٱعْفُ عَنْهُمْ
وَٱسْتَغْفِرْ لَهُمْ وَشَاوِرْهُمْ فِى ٱلْأَمْرِ فَإِذَا عَزَمْتَ فَتَوَكَّلْ عَلَى ٱللَّهِ إِنَّ ٱللَّهَ يُحِبُّ ٱلْمُتَوَكِّلِينَ
(١٥٩)

It is from Allah's Grace that you were gentle with them. Had you been harsh, hardhearted, they would have dispersed from around you. So pardon them, and ask forgiveness for them, and consult them in the conduct of affairs. And when you make a decision, put your trust in Allah; Allah loves the trusting. (Quran 3:159).

We see in the famous hadith of "Ya Ghulam", yet another example of how the Prophet ﷺ is advising a young child, Abdullah ibn Abbas ﷺ about very complex and difficult to understand concepts about life and its workings:

عَنْ عَبْدِ اللَّهِ بْنِ عَبَّاسٍ رَضِيَ اللَّهُ عَنْهُمَا قَالَ: "كُنْت خَلْفَ رَسُولِ اللَّهِ صلى الله عليه و سلم يَوْمًا، فَقَالَ: يَا غُلَامٍ! إِنِّي أُعَلِّمُك كَلِمَاتٍ: احْفَظْ اللَّهَ يَحْفَظْك، احْفَظْ اللَّهَ تَجِدْهُ تُجَاهَك، إذَا سَأَلْت فَاسْأَلْ اللَّهَ، وَإِذَا اسْتَعَنْت فَاسْتَعِنْ بِاَللَّهِ، وَاعْلَمْ أَنَّ الْأُمَّةَ لَوْ اجْتَمَعَتْ عَلَى أَنْ يَنْفَعُوك بِشَيْءٍ لَمْ يَنْفَعُوك إلَّا بِشَيْءٍ قَدْ كَتَبَهُ اللَّهُ لَك، وَإِنْ اجْتَمَعُوا عَلَى أَنْ يَضُرُّوك بِشَيْءٍ لَمْ يَضُرُّوك إلَّا بِشَيْءٍ قَدْ كَتَبَهُ اللَّهُ عَلَيْك؛ رُفِعَتْ الْأَقْلَامُ، وَجَفَّتْ الصُّحُفُ" . رَوَاهُ التِّرْمِذِيُّ [رقم:2516] وَقَالَ: حَدِيثٌ حَسَنٌ صَحِيحٌ. وَفِي رِوَايَةٍ غَيْرِ التِّرْمِذِيِّ: "احْفَظْ اللَّهَ تَجِدْهُ أَمَامك، تَعَرَّفْ إلَى اللَّهِ فِي الرَّخَاءِ يَعْرِفُك فِي الشِّدَّةِ، وَاعْلَمْ أَنَّ مَا أَخْطَأَك لَمْ يَكُنْ لِيُصِيبَك، وَمَا أَصَابَك لَمْ يَكُنْ لِيُخْطِئَك، وَاعْلَمْ أَنَّ النَّصْرَ مَعَ الصَّبْرِ، وَأَنَّ الْفَرَجَ مَعَ الْكَرْبِ، وَأَنَّ مَعَ الْعُسْرِ يُسْرًا."

On the authority of Abu Abbas Abdullah bin Abbas ﷺ who said: One day I was behind the Prophet ﷺ [riding on the same mount] and he said, "O young man, I shall teach you some words [of advice]: Be mindful of Allah and Allah will protect you. Be mindful of Allah and you will find Him in front of you. If you ask, then ask Allah [alone]; and if you seek help, then seek help from Allah [alone]. And know that if the nation were to gather together to benefit you with anything, they would not benefit you except with what Allah had already prescribed for you. And if they were to gather together to harm you with anything, they would not harm you except with what Allah had already prescribed against you. The pens have been lifted and the pages have dried." It was related by at-Tirmidhi, who said it was a good and sound hadeeth. Another narration, other than that of Tirmidhi, reads: Be mindful of Allah, and you will find Him in front of you. Recognize and acknowledge Allah in times of ease and prosperity, and He will remember you in times of adversity. And know that what has passed you by [and you have failed to attain] was not going to befall you, and what has befallen you was not going to pass you by. And know that victory comes with patience, relief with affliction, and hardship with ease.[97]

The approach we see in the examples cited above illustrates the importance of engaging children from a very young age in high level critical thinking skills to develop in them the ability to discern right from wrong and the ability to unpack as life unfolds around them. Adultism reinforces a power imbalance where children are often marginalized, and their needs and contributions are undervalued. As educators and as parents, we must strike a balance between our sense of overprotecting our children because of our love and care for them with the need to train them to the realities of life. The ClassDojo app may make it difficult to strike such a balance.

UC14: Can lead to dysconscious racism

Depicting children as colorful, friendly monsters in ClassDojo may seem harmless but it can lead to the erasure of individual differences.[41] It may seem to align with the democratic ethic of viewing everyone as same; however, in societies where religion and race are intimately tied with one's socioeconomic status, it can lead to inequities. Educators must acknowledge the individual differences in their students and understand how those differences inform their socioeconomic positions so they can implement classroom interventions that are designed to close the academic achievement gap due to these differences.

Some may say that the monsters enable educators to create a color-blind learning environment. In many societies, where whiteness is a normalized privilege, such homogenized monsters may be assumed to be white.[41] Therefore, being color-blind may legitimize whiteness as the assumed norm and may reinforce dysconcious racism within the classroom.

Dysconcious racism refers to the limited or skewed understandings people have about inequity and cultural diversity.[98] These internalized ideologies tend to justify the racial status quo and devalue diversity. These skewed perspectives make it difficult for educators to implement truly equitable educational practices.

Teachers must leverage pedagogical approaches that disrupt the students' internalized ideologies that inform their subjective identities to be truly transformative in successfully negotiating the tensions that arise due to cultural diversity. Even the homogenized innocent monsters of ClassDojo must be viewed through a critical lens to ensure that they do not lead to such skewed racial perspectives and violate children's rights to self-expression and individuality.[41]

Differences among people are an inherent part of the Divine design of Allah's creation and contribute to our sense of belonging while at the same time enabling us to distinguish ourselves from others and should not be disregarded. They become problematic when we attach status and privilege to these differences. This is exactly what Allah ﷻ refers to when He ﷻ says in the Qur'an:

$$\text{يَٰٓأَيُّهَا ٱلنَّاسُ إِنَّا خَلَقۡنَٰكُم مِّن ذَكَرٖ وَأُنثَىٰ وَجَعَلۡنَٰكُمۡ شُعُوبٗا وَقَبَآئِلَ لِتَعَارَفُوٓاْ إِنَّ أَكۡرَمَكُمۡ}$$

$$\text{عِندَ ٱللَّهِ أَتۡقَىٰكُمۡ إِنَّ ٱللَّهَ عَلِيمٌ خَبِيرٞ (١٣)}$$

O people! We created you from a male and a female, and made you races and tribes, that you may know one another. The best among you in the sight of Allah is the most righteous. Allah is All-Knowing, Well-Experienced. (Quran 49:13).

Allah ﷻ uses the word "لِتَعَارَفُوا" (to know one another) as the purpose behind the diversity of humans. In other words, teachers must really get to know their students so they can align their pedagogical approaches to the individual needs of the students. This "getting to know" may involve understanding students' learning preferences, interests, conducting diagnostic assessments to identify where they are in their knowledge and skills, knowing the challenges they may be facing in life, etc. Such knowledge can then be used to design equitable educational practices such as differentiated instruction that can truly address the gaps that may be present due to the diversity in our classrooms.

UC15: Privacy and future data use?

While ClassDojo enables teachers to monitor and analyze student behavior trends in the classroom, its ability to store extensive amounts of student data indefinitely raises privacy concerns, such as the permanence of this data and the potential future applications or interpretations (e.g., misuse, data extrapolation, or teacher biases affecting student development). We are collecting sensitive data from children, a vulnerable group, who cannot provide meaningful consent themselves. We cannot guarantee that this data will be protected, who has control over it, who has access to it, and how it will be used in the future. Many of these apps share data with each other as part of the Internet of Things. This third-party sharing is difficult to control and has serious ethical implications as it is occurring in the backdrop of commercialization of education.

We must be very careful in deploying invasive technologies such as ClassDojo as protection of personal information is an *amanah* (trust) that every individual will be questioned about by Allah ﷻ on the Day of Judgment. The following should be in place as part of upholding this *amanah*:

- A school wide technology plan that provides guidelines on how each technology will be implemented in the school and the classroom taking into consideration the following:
  - Transparency: clearly indicate what data will be collected, how it will be stored, used, and who will have access to it.
  - Data minimization: identify/list the minimal data needed to fulfill the strictly necessary educational purposes.
  - Parental control and access: Parents must control and have full access to any data collected in relation to their children.
  - Legal and ethical standards: Must comply with any Islamic and regulatory requirements.
  - Balanced use: Must prioritize the benefit to children while minimizing any harm.
- Training for teachers and students on the proper and ethical use of technology.
- Since many of these apps extend the school walls to the home, parents should be educated on how to use such technology properly.

It is important for us to carefully evaluate apps like ClassDojo to ensure appropriate safeguards are in place to protect our most vulnerable, our children.

UC16: Disruption of power dynamics

Technology by its very nature is a disruptive force that can rewrite the existing power dynamics. The balance of power is shifting further from nation-states and towards big corporations that are applying surveillance capitalistic logic. This is leading to a corporatocracy where corporate power is the main force driving everything in the digital age. ClassDojo is part of this trend. It has unprecedently collected an immense amount of data on children and is in a unique position to play a strategic role in the development of education policy. Since ClassDojo allows government and educators to leverage social norms at a scale and in a manner unprecedented, what impact does this have on minority cultures, especially of those minorities like us, the Muslims, that are viewed negatively?

Apps like ClassDojo reinforce societal values, norms, and biases that can negatively impact minority cultures, especially Muslims who may be viewed negatively or marginalized in society in several ways:

- **Amplification and reinforcement of negative stereotypes via bias in data collection:** Apps like ClassDojo rely on teachers' assessments to collect student data. With Islamophobia on the rise, teachers can be influenced by implicit biases and unconsciously apply different standards to Muslim students or misinterpret their behavior due to cultural differences and prevalent stereotypes. With ClassDojo sharing data with other apps and potentially using it to inform the further development of the platform and education policy, such biased data can amplify and reinforce negative stereotypes of Islam and Muslims.

- **Conformity to social norms:** Apps like ClassDojo that are developed in the West often promote conformity to Western norms. Muslim students may be expected to behave in ways that may not align with Islamic values making them feel stigmatized and marginalized. For example, a Muslim student fasting the month of Ramadan may feel tired, distracted, or less energetic and can mistakenly be labeled as disengaged or problematic. The cut and paste approach to the adoption of such technologies in Muslim majority countries doesn't mitigate the cross-cultural tensions effectively.

It is important that we address the disruption in power dynamics when such technologies are integrated into our school systems. This begins with identifying all the elements in a school that can be impacted. Then a plan should be developed to mitigate any arising tensions and the negative impact. We should provide cultural sensitivity training to educators where they can understand how such technology can introduce cross-cultural tensions. The integration of the technology should be customized to mitigate any resulting tensions.

Technologies such as ClassDojo can potentially exacerbate the marginalization of Muslims and reinforce negative stereotypes and Islamophobia. It is important for us to become aware of the associated risks so we can take steps to ensure such tools are used in an inclusive and culturally sensitive manner. Our goal should be to establish a school environment where all students feel respected and valued, regardless of their background. By doing so we will ensure that education remains accessible across cultures.

UC17: Does ClassDojo help to establish a sense of online community?

With its overall positive impact on home-school communication, ClassDojo has been identified as helping schools establish a sense of community among all school members.[19] Having all members of the school community use the same platform for communication ensures everyone is getting the same information at the same time, thereby contributing to a sense of community. Teachers are leveraging the app to communicate more with parents and to build home-school partnerships.

There are also unintended consequences of schools relying heavily on one channel of communication:

- Using only one platform to communicate does not indicate that schools are reaching everyone since everyone may not have the same access to technology. Though ClassDojo does tell you how many parents are connected to a classroom, it doesn't tell you how they are connected. They may be connected via a desktop or a mobile device. Some families may simply not have the means to connect. Schools should survey parents to determine their access to technology before deciding to go with one way of communication.

- Some educators are more adept at using this platform than others, which may impact the quality, consistency, and frequency of communication. Schools should provide adequate training to school staff to ensure they are able to use the technology to communicate effectively.

- Communication on ClassDojo is primarily driven by the school; therefore, it is unidirectional. Parents can respond to posts if permission is granted by the school, and they can also send messages to teachers and administrators. Therefore, there is an unequal distribution of power wherein school staff have greater facility in determining how communication unfolds. Schools have a responsibility to ensure parents have more than one channel of communication to advocate for their child.

- Relying heavily on one platform for communication may unintentionally amplify certain narratives over others. What posts parents and the rest of the school community see is determined by what teachers deem worthy of posting since they are the ones who are making the most posts. This informs who/what gets recognized publicly and why and who/what does not. Schools have a responsibility to mitigate the limiting impact on student recognition and promotion of ideas, values, and school culture in general when relying heavily on one platform of communication. They must ensure there are several ways for members of the school community to contribute to the overall school culture.

Home-school communication has been identified as a significant factor in student academic achievement.[10] Schools must establish communication platforms that facilitate the development of learning environments that allow students, parents, and teachers to collaborate effectively in ensuring students' success. ClassDojo greatly facilitates home-school communication but may also lead to a skewed sense of school community that may not necessarily be representative of all school members. Schools must actively find ways to ensure equitable access to the school public forums as they play a critical role in forging the school and student identity and student success.

UC18: Using ClassDojo with very young children

One important question to ask is "when is ClassDojo developmentally appropriate to use?" Perhaps it makes more sense to use ClassDojo in the primary school years since students are expected to learn "school behaviors" and a behavior modification tool, such as the ClassDojo, may be useful in shaping student behavior during these formative years. Teachers are using ClassDojo even in kindergarten classrooms.**Error! Bookmark not defined.** However, I wonder about the impact on young minds on the use of such an invasive technology to "control" their behavior. How does it shape their worldview? What type of motivational reinforcements will they get habituated to? How does it rewire their brains?

Using technologies that focus on monitoring and controlling children behavior through points, rewards, and instant feedback can have far reaching effects on how children perceive themselves, others, and the world around them. Children may come to associate their self-worth with the number of points they have earned, thereby reducing their ability to view success in more holistic ways that define success not only in this life but also in the hereafter. Teachers should carefully curate the concept of success in our classrooms ensuring that it not only encompasses success in this life but also defines success in relation to our life after death.

Instant feedback that is accompanied by superficial rewards reinforces instant gratification making it difficult to remain motivated in difficult tasks that require sustained attention, delayed gratification, and complex problem-solving. Take for example what happens when we make dua during a difficulty. We want Allah ﷻ to respond to our duas immediately. We often do not have the presence of mind to accept that Allah ﷻ may respond to our duas at a time and in a manner that is most suitable for us but may not necessarily meet our expectations. Our children need to have grit and stamina to solve the seemingly insurmountable challenges our ummah is facing. Such grit and stamina must be nurtured in our classrooms via caring and inclusive environments that can motivate our students to rise above the challenges of our times.

Conclusion

In this chapter we have explored many unintended consequences of using ClassDojo. Other technologies also have similar unintended consequences that must be mitigated as they can have significant and often unforeseen effects on us as individuals, communities, and society. If left unchecked, they can undermine our values, and the very goals technology was meant to promote.

Technology is powerful but its impact is unpredictable requiring us to balance innovation with responsibility. By prioritizing ethical use and design and long-term consequences over short-term convenience and profits, we can ensure technology serves us in positive ways. This requires a multifaceted approach to education that integrates critical thinking, digital literacy, emotional intelligence, and a deep connection with the Qur'an. Allah ﷻ presents many examples, scenarios, stories, analogies, and metaphors in the Qur'an to teach us how to successfully navigate this life's challenges. Connecting our children with the Qur'an and the sunnah of the Prophet ﷺ from an early age will empower them to use technology mindfully, critically, and ethically.

7

THE CRITICAL INTEGRATION OF CLASSDOJO IN THE SCHOOL'S EDUCATIONAL LANDSCAPE

Many schools were forced to adopt new technologies during the COVID-19 pandemic. It was an intense period of trial and error driven by an emergency. It forced us to re-evaluate the way teaching and learning occurred in our schools. Often technologies were adopted without giving due consideration to the unintended consequences of technology. Now that we are going back to a level of normalization, it is important that we step back and reassess the use of technology in our schools. Schools should have a well-defined technology plan to ensure the critical and effective use of technology.

A technology plan outlines the goals and objectives of the school's digital roadmap. It leverages technology to facilitate the achievement of the goals that are aligned with the Islamic worldview. It identifies essential processes across the school that can be enhanced with technology. It includes an action plan for the effective adoption of technology across the school along with a budget. It has a plan to train students and staff in the critical and effective use of technology. Lastly it identifies ways to measure progress. A committee ideally comprising of students, teachers, parents, Islamic scholars, and experts in the field should develop and own the technology plan.

Technology Plan Outline

There are many technology plan templates out there. Schools can use the following outline adapted from a technology plan template from Emily Miller for her master's thesis to develop their technology plan:[99]

1. **Mission/Vision Statement:** A school's mission defines the school's goals and objectives and the approach to achieve them. A vision statement highlights the desired position of the school. Here are some questions to consider:
    a. Does my school already have a mission/vision statement? If yes, then how does it guide the integration of technology in the school?
    b. Does my school have a strategic plan? If so, how does this technology plan connect to it?
    c. How does my technology plan align with the principles and goals of *tarbiyah*?
    d. What kind of digital identity do we want our school, staff, and students to have?
    e. What motivates us to embrace change and to adopt new ways of doing things? Are these motivations aligned with the goals and values in Islam?
2. **Tech Committee:** identify the core group of people who will take ownership of the technology plan and ensure its

implementation and continuous development. Here are some guiding questions:

    a.   What is the scope of the committee? What are their duties and responsibilities? Who will they report to? What is the recruitment process?

    b.   Have we included all stakeholders (teachers, support staff, students, parents, administrators, experts, board members, Islamic scholars, etc.)?

    c.   How often and where will they meet?

    d.   What are the deliverables? How will they communicate their work with the school community?

3. **Guiding Principles:** What are the frameworks, standards, and best practices guiding the use of technology in our school? Some things to consider:

    a.   How do the principles of *tarbiyah* inform the use of technology in our school?

    b.   How can we use the ISTE Standards to guide the use of technology in our school?[100]

    c.   Are there any related guidelines from government agencies and advocacy organizations that should be integrated?

    d.   What are our goals for the integration of technology? Is there a balance between technology as a goal versus technology to achieve our goals?

4. **Needs Assessment and Analysis:** The following user surveys should be conducted:

    a.   A survey of key stakeholders to understand their feelings, current capabilities, and commitments.

    b.   A survey of the current state of technology adoption and integration in the school.

These can be done through online surveys, focus group discussions, document analysis, observations, etc. Questions to consider:

    a. Which different stakeholders should be targeted for surveys?

    b. What is the best way to understand and document the needs on the ground?

    c. What does the data indicate?

5. **School Infrastructure:** The plan should capture the status of the technology infrastructure in the school. This not only includes the hardware but also the policies and procedures that guide the school wide adoption and integration of technology. Having a better understanding of the status on the ground will help to make informed decisions. Some questions to consider include:

    a. What technology and infrastructure to support current technology and future technologies is currently available in the school?

    b. What is the student to device and teacher to device ratio?

    c. What digital resources are currently in use?

    d. What guidelines, policies, and procedures are in place to ensure the effective implementation and integration of technology? Is there a maintenance plan for technology?

    e. What type of IT support is available in the school for teachers and students?

6. **Plan and Procedure:** Identify all the related goals and how the school can achieve them. Each goal should have a timeline, resources to support, identifiable outcomes, and a plan to collect evidence to determine achievement of goals (Key Performance Indicators). Some questions to consider include:

a.	How does this align with the school's strategic plan?

b.	How will buy in among targeted users be achieved for new technologies?

c.	What supports will be needed to ensure effective adoption and integration of technology?

d.	What are the academic targets and goals we intend to achieve through this technology plan?

e.	What evidence will let us know we are achieving these academic targets? How will this be collected and communicated?

f.	How will we track progress?

g.	Is the timeline realistic? Is there sufficient allocation of resources (budget, etc.) to achieve the plan?

h.	Will the plan be reviewed periodically for any revisions and adjustments?

7.	**Community Resources and Support:** Identify all the resources available within the school and in the community that can help to ensure the success of the technology plan. Create a budget to identify all the financial resources needed and the sources of funding. Some questions to consider include:

a.	What funding is needed to achieve the goals of the technology plan?

b.	What funding sources are available in the school (school budget) and in the community (government grants, businesses, *masajid*, community organizations, etc.)? Who are all the stakeholders (parent support team, student council, community leaders, parents, etc.) that can help in acquiring these funds?

c.	How will the budget be submitted, approved, and communicated to the community?

ClassDojo as part of the School Technology Plan

ClassDojo and any other app that is intended to be adopted in our school should go through a careful evaluation process. We explored many themes while analyzing the use of ClassDojo and its impact on us. I've used these themes to develop a rubric to evaluate ClassDojo to determine its use in an educational environment. This rubric can also be used to evaluate other apps and e-learning tools.

Table 4: App & e-tools Evaluation Rubric

3-Works Well 2-Minor Concerns 1-Serious Concerns		3	2	1	N/A
#	Criteria				
1	Aligns with the Islamic worldview				
2	Affordances of the app align with the academic goals				
3	Doesn't disrupt existing power structure(s)				
4	Doesn't promote a materialistic lifestyle				
5	Privacy of users is maintained				
6	User data is not shared with third parties without consent				
7	Data is safe				
8	A clear data deletion and retention policy is available				
9	User data is tracked and stored				
10	Any unintended consequences can be mitigated with minimal effort				
11	Can be scaled up or down to accommodate any group size				
12	Easy to use. Requires minimal effort to become skillful users.				
13	Technical support and help is available.				
14	The app/tool can be used by diverse learners				
15	Does not require any special equipment or additional infrastructure to operate.				
16	Cost is within the budget				
17	The app/tool can be integrated with other apps/tools used in the school.				
18	The app/tool can be used on a variety of platforms.				
19	Doesn't require a user login. Personal user information is not collected.				
20	Users can decide how their data is to be shared.				
21	Users can save their data in a variety of ways/formats				

3-Works Well 2-Minor Concerns 1-Serious Concerns	3	2	1	N/A
#	Criteria			
22	The tool can be customized to align with the values and needs of the school.				
23	The tool is widely known. It's likely most learners will be familiar with it.				
24	User data can be tracked to identify and mitigate learning gaps.				
25	Facilitates higher order thinking skills.				
26	Facilitates metacognitive skills				
27	Teachers can provide feedback easily.				

Suggestions for Educators

1. Usually, majority of students tend to follow classroom expectations. So, use ClassDojo for only those students who need to be redirected more frequently than others. Have a contract of agreement between the teacher and the students/parents and discuss the rationale for using this only with them beforehand.

2. If using ClassDojo, keep a close eye on any negative impact of the game-based point system on student motivation and be ready to modify as needed.

3. ClassDojo should not be the only tool in a teacher's arsenal to redirect and to motivate students. Teachers should use a variety of strategies to redirect and motivate students. These include smiling at them, praising them verbally, talking with them about their behavior, and building relationships of trust and care that would enable them to inspire their students to do better.

4. Turn off the notification sounds whether for positive or negative points to avoid distraction or de-motivation and to maintain the discreetness required of a Muslim in correcting another Muslims mistake.

5. Do not display points on the screen to avoid embarrassing and distracting students. Moreover, students will be more focused on earning the points than on their learning if the points are on full display.

6. Reflect on the reasons for students' disruptive behavior and allocate time to individually discuss the disruptive behaviour with students.

7. Reset behavior points at specified intervals throughout the year. Guide students to reflect on their progress during each interval and ways to close any gaps. The length of these intervals can be adjusted according to the age of the students with younger students having shorter intervals. This will bring the focus back on using reflection to improve behavior and to close any achievement gaps.

8. Create a category for *taubah* points. Students can achieve these points by performing certain acts of *taubah* (saying *astaghfar* certain number of times, acts of kindness, praying two *raka'ahs*, etc.). These can then be used towards the points total.

9. Use behavior management plans customized for individual students to guide them to meet expectations.

10. Familiarize parents with the limitations of the point system and the negative potential influence on students. More importantly, speak with parents to provide more details regarding their child's infractions rather than just a notification about points being deducted.

11. Use anonymous avatars to avoid putting students on the spot and to protect their privacy. This ensures the privacy and security of students' data since the app mostly resides on mobile devices whose security can be compromised easily.

12. Do not lose sight of the big picture: Student-teacher relationships are the most influential in motivating students; therefore, focus on that first before spending time on reactive approaches such as redirecting students.

Conclusion

ClassDojo's integrated points system, embedded class activities, customizable avatars, class e-Portfolio system, and the ease of communication via a social platform "secure" community make an appealing package for many teachers and school administrators. Like the adoption of most technology, the pace at which ClassDojo has been adopted in schools has not allowed us to critically evaluate its impact on teaching and learning and on our Muslim identity. This book has allowed us to hit the pause button so we can take a step back and reflect on the adoption of such invasive technologies and their impact on us.

Throughout this book we have explored many important themes associated with the use of ClassDojo and similar technologies:

- We have looked at how ClassDojo and similar technologies are intentionally being black boxed to serve specific agendas and how those agendas disrupt the goals of *tarbiyah* and further marginalize Muslims.

- We have scrutinized the theoretical foundations of ClassDojo that are mostly derived from a very secular and materialistic framework. They do not centralize the role of Allah ﷻ as the Source of all knowledge and guidance and the belief in the Hereafter as the motivation behind all our actions.

- We have examined how belief in the liberating possibilities of technology is giving rise to new faiths such as dataism that are at odds with the Islamic worldview and way of life.

- With increasing datafication of our lives, data has become the most valuable resource leading to datamining as the primary motive behind most of the free apps like ClassDojo that are silently indoctrinating our children into a culture of surveillance. This has raised important ethical and privacy concerns. We studied Islamic notions on privacy and how they can help us successfully negotiate this loss in privacy.

- Datafication further amplifies Islamophobia. ClassDojo has many inherent biases that subvert the goals of education in Islam. We outlined the digital literacies teachers must have and teach students to successfully mitigate the negative impact of such invasive technologies.

- Teachers have adopted ClassDojo because it helps them with classroom management. The token economy system in ClassDojo is reductionist in its approach to character development. We covered many proactive classroom management strategies that teachers can integrate to establish a culture of care and love that can forge an identity that is closely connected with Allah ﷻ and the way of the Prophet ﷺ.

- ClassDojo's aim is character development through the positive psychology movement, the growth mindset, and socio-emotional learning. Many of these concepts do not align with the *fitrah* of the human being and with the approach to character development as modeled to us by the Prophet ﷺ. Teachers must be trained in these core concepts of character development so they can establish a classroom environment that nurtures the Muslim identity.

- ClassDojo, like most technologies, has many unintended consequences. Educators must take a critical and reflective approach to using technology to anticipate and mitigate the tensions that arise due to the integration of technology in our lives. The technology plan outline provided can help us in the strategic adoption of technology in our schools.

Muslim educators have a duty to create a school and classroom environment that centralizes the Islamic worldview and the way of the Prophet ﷺ in the development of the Muslim identity in our children. Islamic and digital literacy is essential to becoming critical consumers of technology and in confidently negotiating the many tensions of living as a Muslim in an increasingly hostile, pluralistic, globalized, and digital world. This is the best defense against such disruptive technologies like ClassDojo. I encourage you to use the many discussions, strategies, and tools in this book to develop the Islamic mindset and to implement the Islamic environment in our classrooms and schools that can help us and our students to remain steadfast on the path to virtue (the Straight Path) in an increasingly digitized world.

GLOSSARY

 (Sallallahu alaihi wasallam) – May Allah's peace and blessings be upon him. It is a prayer Muslims make for Prophet Muhammad whenever he is mentioned.

 (Jalla jalalahu) – May Allah be glorified.

 (Radiallahu anhu) – May Allah be pleased with him

Amanah (أمانة) – The concept of trust, honesty, and responsibility in Islam.

Astaghfar (أستغفر الله) – Means to say أستغفر الله (I seek forgiveness from Allah) to ask Allah for pardon for our sins and shortcomings. It is a form of remembrance of Allah .

Big Data – We are generating an unprecedented amount of data as individuals and groups connected via devices and sensors. Big data refers to these vast and intricate datasets that surpass the ability of conventional data processing tools to manage, store, and analyze effectively. These datasets are characterized by the **three Vs:**[31] **1. Volume:** The vast volume of data produced and collected, often spanning from terabytes to petabytes or beyond. **2. Velocity:** The rate at which data is created, gathered, and processed in real-time or close to it. **3. Variety:** The wide variety of data types and sources, encompassing structured, semi-structured, and unstructured data. Big data analytics is the process of extracting valuable insights and patterns from large and complex datasets.

California Consumer Privacy Act (CCPA) – A California state law that enhances privacy rights and consumer protection for residents of California. Enacted in January 2020, the CCPA gives Californians more control over their personal information.

Children's Online Privacy Protection Act (COPPA) – A U.S. federal law to protect the privacy and personal information of children under the age of 13.

Du'a (دعاء) – The Arabic word for supplication or prayer in Islam.

Epistemological – Refers to epistemology, a branch of philosophy concerned with the theory of knowledge. It deals with questions about the nature, scope, and limits of human knowledge, including how we come to know things, what justifies beliefs, and the distinction between belief and knowledge.

Family Educational Rights and Privacy Acts (FERPA) – A U.S. federal law enacted in 1974 to protect the privacy of student education records.

Fitrah (فطرة) – refers to the pure, untainted, innocent, God given disposition or inherent state with which all humans are born.

General Data Protection Regulation (GDPR) – A comprehensive data protection law enacted by the European Union in May 2018. It aims to enhance individuals' rights regarding their personal data and establish strict guidelines for how organizations collect, store, and process that data.

Hajj (حج) – One of the Five Pillars of Islam that refers to the pilgrimage journey to Makkah that should be undertaken by all physically and financially capable Muslim adults. The journey must be taken during the Islamic month of Dhul Hijjah and involves a series of rituals.

Halal (حلال) – An Islamic concept that refers to anything that is permissible or lawful.

Humanism – a worldview that emphasizes the value, dignity, and agency of human beings in contrast to supernatural or religious explanations for human life and existence. It is typically a secular stance that centralizes the power of human reason over Divine guidance.

'Ibadah (عبادة) – Means worship, servitude, and devotion to Allah. In Islam it refers to both the religious rituals as well as all actions, deeds, and behaviors that are done in accordance with Allah's ﷻ commands and to seek His ﷻ pleasure.

Ihsan (إحسان) – The concept of excellence or perfection in our actions. It means striving to do our best in seeking to achieve the highest level of devotion to Allah ﷻ. It is a central concept in Islam that serves as a guiding principle for personal conduct, worship, and interactions with others.

Internet of Things (IoT) – Describes a system of interconnected devices, objects, and systems that can communicate and exchange data autonomously, without direct human involvement. These devices are equipped with sensors, actuators, and communication features, enabling them to gather and send data over the Internet or other networks. The data gathered by these devices is transmitted to central platforms or cloud-based systems for processing, analysis, and interpretation.

Jibril - The Archangel Gabriel and in Islam is the leader of all the angels and plays a crucial role in conveying the Diving message and guidance to the prophets and messengers.

Khalifa (خليفة) – An Arabic term that translates to "successor" or "representative" and refers to our role as Allah's vicegerents or stewards in this life. It is a foundational concept that informs Islamic ethics and emphasizes our responsibility to manage and care for Allah's creation.

Kiraaman kaatibin (كِرامًا كَاتِبِينَ) – Means "honorable scribes" and refers to the two angels that are assigned by Allah ﷻ to record the good and bad deeds of all humans.

Ludic surveillance – Collection of user data and monitoring through games and entertainment systems.

Machiavellian tendencies – Behaviors or personality traits that are manipulative, deceitful, and self-serving to increase one's power and control at the expense of others.

Mahram (مَحرَم) – A concept in Islam that refers to a person with whom marriage is permanently forbidden due to blood ties, breastfeeding (foster relationships), and marriage ties (in-laws, etc.). Opposite genders that are mahram to each other can have physical and social interactions without the need for modesty restrictions like hijab, as they are considered part of their intimate family circle. This helps define the social interaction boundaries thereby ensuring the preservation of modesty and the family structure in Islam. A ***non-Mahram*** would be anyone who is not related by blood or marriage with whom marriage is permissible.

Masajid (مساجد) – Plural of masjid, the Arabic term for a mosque.

Metadata – Data about data. It provides us details about the characteristics, context, and structure of data. It helps us to organize, manage, understand, and preserve data.

Murabbih (مُرَبِّيَه) – Refers to a mentor, educator, trainer, and a role model. It is someone who guides, nurtures, educates, and develops the character, knowledge, and faith of others.

Postphenomenology – An approach within the field of philosophy that builds on phenomenology but emphasizes the role of technology in shaping human experiences and perceptions. It examines how our interactions with technological artifacts influence our understanding of the world and ourselves. Instead of focusing solely on human consciousness and subjective experience and technologies as merely functional and instrumental objects, postphenomenology considers the relationships between humans and technologies, exploring how these interactions co-construct our realities.

Raka'ahs (رَكْعَة) – One unit or cycle of *salah* (prayer) in Islam.

Saint-Simonian – Followers of Saint-Simon, the 18th century French social theorist, who advocated for a more efficient and equitable social order by empowering industrialists, scientists, and other skilled professionals.

Shari'ah (شريعة) – Refers to the Islamic law or the Divine law derived from the Qur'an, the teachings of Prophet Muhammad ﷺ, consensus of Islamic scholars (Ijma), and analogical reasoning (Qiyas).

Shaytan (شيطان) – Commonly spelled Satan, in Islam, *shaytan* is a *jinn* (another creation of Allah made from smokeless fire). He is a Divinely cursed rebellious being who has taken an oath to lead humans away from the path of righteousness and the worship of Allah ﷻ.

Sunnah (سنة) – Refers to the actions, sayings, approvals, and practices of Prophet Muhammad ﷺ that serve as a model for Muslims to follow.

Surah (سورة) – Refers to a chapter in the Qur'an.

Tahara (طهارة) – The concept of physical and spiritual purity and cleanliness in Islam.

Taqwa (تقوى) – A central concept in Islam that refers to mindfulness and awareness of Allah ﷻ in all aspects of our life. It means to live in accordance with Allah's ﷻ guidance, avoiding actions that displease Him ﷻ, and doing our best to fulfill His ﷻ commands with sincerity and devotion. The Arabic term is often translated as "piety" or "God-consciousness".

Tarbiyah (تربية) – The holistic and comprehensive development of the individual in all aspects of life; physical, intellectual, socio-emotional, moral, and spiritual. Tarbiyah is more than formal education. It is the cultivation of good character, ethical values, proper behavior, and a strong connection to Allah ﷻ, the Prophet ﷺ, self, family, and society.

Tawakkul (تَوَكُّل) – The concept of trust and reliance on Allah ﷻ while taking all the necessary actions and making efforts toward achieving the target or overcoming the difficulty.

Tawbah (توبة) – A concept in Islam that refers to the act of repentance or returning to Allah after committing a sin or wrongdoing.

Ummah (أمة) – The global community of Muslims bound together by a shared belief. Islamic concept that represents the collective identity, solidarity, and responsibility among Muslims irrespective of one's location, national identity, or cultural background.

Wasatiyyah (الوَسَطِيَّة) – It means observing a balanced, moderate, and just approach in all aspects of life with reference to Islamic teachings.

Wudu (وضوء) – Also known as ablution, it is the ritual washing performed by Muslims to cleanse themselves physically and spiritually before engaging in Salah (prayer), reading the Qur'an, and other religious acts.

Zakah (زكاة) – One of the Five Pillars of Islam that refers to the obligatory almsgiving or charity that Muslims who possess wealth above a certain threshold are required to give to the needy.

Zone of Proximal Development (ZPD) – An idea proposed by the Russian psychologist, Lev Vygotsky, ZPD is the level between what a learner can do independently on their own and what they cannot do, even with assistance. The complexity of tasks is at a level that requires learners to complete them with the assistance of a more knowledgeable other.

NOTES

[1] Saleem, M. M. (2009). An exploratory study of the implementation of computer technology in an American Islamic private school [Ph.D., The University of Wisconsin - Madison]. https://www.proquest.com/docview/305033887/abstract/EA70 D7BF7DF64EA1PQ/1

[2] Yuen, C. L. (2021). *Exploring Teachers' Experiences of Using ClassDojo: A Postphenomenological Study* [Ph.D., University of Alberta]. https://doi.org/10.7939/r3-swxn-4822

[3] ClassDojo. (n.d.). *ClassDojo*. ClassDojo. Retrieved December 11, 2024, from https://www.classdojo.com/

[4] Baalsrud Hauge, J., C S Cardoso, J., Roque, L., & Gonzalez-Calero, P. A. (2021). A Review on the Contribution of ClassDojo as Point System Gamification in Education. In *Entertainment Computing— ICEC 2021* (Vol. 13056). Springer International Publishing AG.

[5] Williamson, B. (2017). Decoding ClassDojo: Psycho-policy, social-emotional learning and persuasive educational technologies. *Learning, Media and Technology, 42*(4), 440–453. https://doi.org/10.1080/17439884.2017.1278020

[6] ClassDojo Recognized in Fast Company 2016 Innovation by Design Awards. (2016). *PR Newswire Association LLC.*

[7] Benhadj, Y., Messaoudi, M. E., & Nfissi, A. (2019). Artificial Intelligence in Education: Integrating Serious Gaming into the Language Class ClassDojo Technology for Classroom Behavioral Management. *IAES International Journal of Artificial Intelligence, 8*(4), 382–390.

[8] Bahceci, F. (2019). CLASSDOJO: The Effects of Digital Classroom Management Program on Students-Parents and Teachers. *International Online Journal of Educational Sciences, 11*(4), 160–180.

[9] Watters, A. (2015, February 4). *The Automatic Teacher*. Hack Education. http://hackeducation.com/2015/02/04/the-automatic-teacher

[10] Love, D. J. (2022). *ClassDojo New Age Classroom Management* [Ed.D., The Chicago School of Professional Psychology]. https://www.proquest.com/docview/2664439242/abstract/2467 FEDBAD9B4F53PQ/1

[11] Tough, P. (2016, May 17). How Kids Learn Resilience. *The Atlantic*. https://www.theatlantic.com/magazine/archive/2016/06/how-kids-really-succeed/480744/

[12] *KIPP Public Charter Schools*. (n.d.). KIPP Public Charter Schools. Retrieved August 25, 2024, from https://www.kipp.org/

[13] *The Heckman Equation*. (n.d.). The Heckman Equation. Retrieved August 30, 2024, from https://heckmanequation.org/the-heckman-equation/

[14] *Angela Duckworth*. (n.d.). Positive Psychology Center. Retrieved August 30, 2024, from https://ppc.sas.upenn.edu/people/angela-duckworth

[15] Green, E. (2010, March 2). Building a Better Teacher. *The New York Times*. https://www.nytimes.com/2010/03/07/magazine/07Teachers-t.html

[16] Canter, L., & Canter, M. (2001). Assertive Discipline: Positive Behavior Management for Today's Classroom. Canter & Associates.

[17] Busso, D. S., & Pollack, C. (2015). No brain left behind: Consequences of neuroscience discourse for education. *Learning, Media and Technology, 40*(2), 168–186. https://doi.org/10.1080/17439884.2014.908908

[18] Ibn Al-Jawzi, A.-H. A.-F. (n.d.). *The Devil's Deception. A complete translation of the classical text Talbis Iblis* (A. Khalid, Trans.). Dar as-Sunnah Publishers. Retrieved December 12, 2024, from https://www.kalamullah.com/the-devils-deception.html

19 Lampert, L. L. (2020). *ClassDojo and Home-School Communication* [Ed.D., New Jersey City University]. https://www.proquest.com/docview/2627082551/abstract/E804 696B4BE34A46PQ/1

20 Wolf, P. J. (2015*). Class Dojo: An awesome progress monitoring tool!* Georgia Association for Positive Behavior Support Conference, Georgia, USA. https://digitalcommons.georgiasouthern.edu/gapbs/2015/2015/13/

21 Singer, N. (2014). ClassDojo Adopts Deletion Policy for Student Data. *New York Times (Online).*

22 Robacker, C. M., Rivera, C. J., & Warren, S. H. (2016). A Token Economy Made Easy Through ClassDojo. *Intervention in School and Clinic, 52*(1), 39–43. https://doi.org/10.1177/1053451216630279

23 Brown, A. W. (2021). *ClassDojo and the Effects of Gamification on Student Engagement within the Third-Grade Art Classroom: An Action Research Study* [Ed.D., University of South Carolina]. https://www.proquest.com/docview/2673577310/abstract/AE9 5ED4C8CBF47C4PQ/1

24 Wilson, R. M. (2017). *Classdojo.com: The Effects of a Digital Classroom Management Program* [Ed.D., Trevecca Nazarene University]. https://www.proquest.com/docview/1916555633/abstract/C538 E9F16BDD46BFPQ/1

25 Fenwick, T., & Edwards, R. (2010). *Actor-Network Theory in Education.* Routledge. https://doi.org/10.4324/9780203849088

26 Shechtman, N., DeBarger H., A., Dornsife, C., Rosier, S., & Yarnall, L. (2013). *Promoting Grit, Tenacity and Perseverance: Critical Factors for Success in the 21st Century.* U.S. Department of Education Office of Educational Technology. https://www.flstopcccoalition.org/files/F6A22756-73E4-4406-BC0F-F9E8340A37C6--E36F73DA-E434-44F5-B829-1C27BAA8532F/grit-tenacity-and-perseverance-feb-2013-doe.pdf

27 Mays, S. (2017, March 18). Homo Deus: Dataism [Blog]. *Smays.Com.* https://www.smays.com/2017/03/homodeus2/

28 Harari, Y. N. (2016). *Homo Deus: A Brief History of Tomorrow*. Harvill Secker.

29 Dijck, J. van. (2014). Datafication, dataism and dataveillance: Big Data between scientific paradigm and ideology. *Surveillance & Society, 12*(2), 197–208. https://doi.org/10.24908/ss.v12i2.4776

30 Mills, C. (2019, October 16). The rise of dataism [Blog]. *Hult International Business School*. https://www.hult.edu/blog/the-rise-of-dataism/

31 Brooks, D. (2013, February 5). Opinion | The Philosophy of Data. *The New York Times*. https://www.nytimes.com/2013/02/05/opinion/brooks-the-philosophy-of-data.html

32 Barabási, A.-L. (2022, September 23). Why the World Needs 'Dataism,' the New Art Movement That Helps Us Understand How Our World Is Shaped by Big Data. *Artnet News*. https://news.artnet.com/art-world-archives/introducing-dataism-2181005

33 Manioudakis, S. (2023, August 28). *Dataism: Idea or Ideology?* HackerNoon. https://hackernoon.com/dataism-idea-or-ideology

34 *Hadith 25, 40 Hadith Qudsi—Forty Hadith Qudsi—Sunnah.com—Sayings and Teachings of Prophet Muhammad* (صلى الله عليه و سلم). (n.d.). Retrieved December 4, 2024, from https://sunnah.com/qudsi40:25

35 *Hadith 3592 Sunan Abi Dawud*. (n.d.). Sunnah.Com. Retrieved October 5, 2024, from https://sunnah.com/abudawud:3592

36 Qureshi, H. (2023, May 16). *Harnessing the Power of Big Data in Islam*. Linkedin. https://www.linkedin.com/pulse/harnessing-power-big-data-islam-humayun-qureshi

37 Mayer-Schönberger, V., & Cukier, K. (2013). *Big Data: A Revolution That Will Transform How We Live, Work, and Think*. Houghton Mifflin Harcourt.

38 Parton, S. (2018, September 30). The Rise of Dataism: A Threat to Freedom or a Scientific Revolution? *Singularity Hub*.

https://singularityhub.com/2018/09/30/the-rise-of-dataism-a-threat-to-freedom-or-a-scientific-revolution/

[39] O'Connor, B., Balasubramanyan, R., Routledge, B., & Smith, N. (2010). *From Tweets to Polls: Linking Text Sentiment to Public Opinion Time Series. 11.*

[40] *Common Sense Privacy Evaluation for ClassDojo.* (2022, October 3). Commonsense.Org. https://privacy.commonsense.org/evaluation/classdojo

[41] Garlen, J., Professor, A., Childhood, Studies, Y., & University, C. (2019, February 26). ClassDojo raises concerns about children's rights. *The Canadian Press.* https://www.proquest.com/docview/2186811998/citation/D2B863AC44DD4B11PQ/1

[42] *Data Deletion and Retention.* (n.d.). ClassDojo Help Center. Retrieved August 22, 2024, from https://help.classdojo.com/hc/en-us/articles/203730319-Data-Deletion-and-Retention

[43] Soroko, A. (2016). No child left alone: The ClassDojo app. *Our Schools/Our Selves.*

[44] Friedli, L., & Stearn, R. (2015). Positive affect as coercive strategy: Conditionality, activation and the role of psychology in UK government workfare programmes. *Medical Humanities, 41*(1), 40–47. https://doi.org/10.1136/medhum-2014-010622

[45] Risen, J., & Wingfield, N. (2013, June 20). Web's Reach Binds N.S.A. and Silicon Valley Leaders. *The New York Times.* https://www.nytimes.com/2013/06/20/technology/silicon-valley-and-spy-agency-bound-by-strengthening-web.html

[46] Zuboff, S. (2019). *The Age of Surveillance Capitalism: The Fight for a Human Future at the New Frontier of Power.* PublicAffairs.

[47] Khan, A. (2021, June 16). When Data Privacy Becomes a Subject of Faith [Blog]. *YES! Magazine.* https://www.yesmagazine.org/social-justice/2021/06/16/app-data-collection-muslims-in-tech

[48] Saputra, A. A., Fasa, M. I., & Ambarwati, D. (2022). Islamic-Based Digital Ethics: The Phenomenon of Online Consumer Data Security. *Share: Jurnal Ekonomi Dan Keuangan Islam, 11*(1), Article 1. https://doi.org/10.22373/share.v11i1.11167

[49] *Muslims in Canada Data Initiative (MiCDI)*. (n.d.). [Institute of Islamic Studies University of Toronto]. MiCDI. Retrieved September 13, 2024, from https://www.micdi.ca/about

[50] Alshech, E. (2004). "Do Not Enter Houses Other than Your Own": The Evolution of the Notion of a Private Domestic Sphere in Early Sunnī Islamic Thought. *Islamic Law and Society, 11*(3), 291–332.

[51] Association for Computing Machinery. (2018). *ACM Code of Ethics and Professional Conduct.* https://www.acm.org/code-of-ethics

[52] Maududi, S. A. A. (1988). An-Nur 24:27-34—Tafhim ul Quran (Z. I. Ansari, Trans.). In *Towards Understanding the Quran-English version of Tafhim ul Quran.* The Islamic Foundation. https://islamicstudies.info/tafheem.php?sura=24&verse=27&to=34

[53] Bakhrudin, B., Margolang, F., Sudarmanto, E., & Sugiono, S. (2023). Islamic Perspectives on Cybersecurity and Data Privacy: Legal and Ethical Implications. *West Science Law and Human Rights, 1,* 166–172. https://doi.org/10.58812/wslhr.v1i04.323

[54] an-Nawawi, Y. ibn S. (n.d.). Book 5: Book of Greetings Hadith 27. In *Riyad as-Salihin* (Vol. 5). Retrieved November 5, 2024, from https://www.islamicity.org/hadith/search/index.php?q=37359&sss=1

[55] an-Nawawi, Y. ibn S. (n.d.). Book 5: The Book of Greetings. In *Riyad as-Salihin* (1–5). Retrieved November 5, 2024, from https://sunnah.com/riyadussalihin/5

[56] Elias, A. A. (2014, May 19). *Hadith on Sins: Allah forgives everyone but sinners in public* [Blog]. Daily Hadith Online. https://www.abuaminaelias.com/dailyhadithonline/2014/05/19/allah-forgives-everyone-except-shameless/

[57] International Society for Technology in Education. (n.d.). *ISTE Standards: For Students* [International Society for Technology in Education]. ISTE. Retrieved September 24, 2024, from https://iste.org/standards/students

[58] *The Digital Use Divide.* (n.d.). Office of Educational Technology. Retrieved September 24, 2024, from https://tech.ed.gov/netp/digital-use-divide/

[59] International Society for Technology in Education. (n.d.-b). *ISTE Standards: For Educators.* ISTE. Retrieved September 24, 2024, from https://iste.org/standards/educators

[60] Ford, W. B., Radley, K. C., Tingstrom, D. H., Dart, E. H., & Dufrene, B. (2022). Evaluation of the Good Behavior Game Using ClassDojo in Secondary Classrooms. *School Psychology Review, 0*(0), 1–15. https://doi.org/10.1080/2372966X.2022.2067736

[61] Robacker, C. M., Rivera, C. J., & Warren, S. H. (2016). A Token Economy Made Easy Through ClassDojo. *Intervention in School and Clinic, 52*(1), 39–43. https://doi.org/10.1177/1053451216630279

[62] Wachendorf, M. (2017). *A Comparative Study of Traditional Token Economies and ClassDojo* [M.S.Ed., Western Illinois University]. https://www.proquest.com/docview/1927483861/abstract/5435 8CC12FE34D26PQ/1

[63] Resetar Volz, J. L., & Cook, C. R. (2009). Group-Based Preference Assessment for Children and Adolescents in a Residential Setting: Examining Developmental, Clinical, Gender, and Ethnic Differences. *Behavior Modification, 33*(6), 778–794. https://doi.org/10.1177/0145445509348733

[64] Akin-Little, K. A., & Little, S. G. (2004). Re-Examining the Overjustification Effect. *Journal of Behavioral Education, 13*(3), 179–192.

[65] Donaldson, J. M., Vollmer, T. R., Krous, T., Downs, S., & Berard, K. P. (2011). An Evaluation of the Good Behavior Game in Kindergarten Classrooms. *Journal of Applied Behavior Analysis, 44*(3), 605–609. https://doi.org/10.1901/jaba.2011.44-605

66 Kellam, S. G., Mackenzie, A. C. L., Brown, C. H., Poduska, J. M., Wang, W., Petras, H., & Wilcox, H. C. (2011). The good behavior game and the future of prevention and treatment. *Addiction Science & Clinical Practice, 6*(1), 73–84.

67 Lipscomb, A. H., Anderson, M., & Gadke, D. L. (2018). Comparing the effects of ClassDojo with and without Tootling intervention in a postsecondary special education classroom setting. *Psychology in the Schools, 55*(10), 1287–1301. https://doi.org/10.1002/pits.22185

68 Darling-Hammond, L., Flook, L., Cook-Harvey, C., Barron, B., & Osher, D. (2020). Implications for educational practice of the science of learning and development. *Applied Developmental Science, 24*(2), 97–140. https://doi.org/10.1080/10888691.2018.1537791

69 Gresham, F. (2015). Evidence-Based Social Skills Interventions for Students at Risk for EBD. *Remedial and Special Education, 36*(2), 100–104. https://doi.org/10.1177/0741932514556183

70 Kasson, E. M., & Wilson, A. N. (2016). Preliminary Evidence on the Efficacy of Mindfulness Combined with Traditional Classroom Management Strategies. *Behavior Analysis in Practice, 10*(3), 242–251. https://doi.org/10.1007/s40617-016-0160-x

71 Madigan, J. (2019, January 14). How Video Games Do Feedback Well (and Poorly). *The Psychology of Video Games.* https://www.psychologyofgames.com/2019/01/how-video-games-do-feedback-well-and-poorly/

72 Maslow, A. H. (1943). A theory of human motivation. *Psychological Review, 50*(4), 370–396. https://doi.org/10.1037/h0054346

73 Deci, E. L., & Ryan, R. M. (1985). *Intrinsic Motivation and Self-Determination in Human Behavior.* Springer US. https://doi.org/10.1007/978-1-4899-2271-7

74 Vroom, V. H. (1994). *Work and Motivation.* Wiley. https://www.wiley.com/en-us/Work+and+Motivation-p-9780787900304

75 Locke, E., & Latham, G. (2002). Building a practically useful theory of goal setting and task motivation—A 35-year odyssey. *The*

American Psychologist, 57, 705–717. https://doi.org/10.1037//0003-066X.57.9.705

[76] Weiner, B. (1985). An attributional theory of achievement motivation and emotion. *Psychological Review, 92*(4), 548–573. https://doi.org/10.1037/0033-295X.92.4.548

[77] Bandura, A. (1978). Self-efficacy: Toward a unifying theory of behavioral change. *Advances in Behaviour Research and Therapy, 1*(4), 139–161. https://doi.org/10.1016/0146-6402(78)90002-4

[78] Hull, C. L. (1943). *Principles Of Behavior.* http://archive.org/details/in.ernet.dli.2015.205891

[79] Skinner, B. F. (Burrhus F. with Internet Archive). (1953). *Science and human behavior.* Macmillan. http://archive.org/details/sciencehumanbeha0000skin_p4g5

[80] an-Nawawi, Y. ibn S. (n.d.-c). The Book of Miscellany. In *Riyad as-Salihin.* Retrieved November 10, 2024, from https://sunnah.com/riyadussalihin:387

[81] Horn, J. (2014, November 17). ClassDojo: Another Insecure Child Labeling, Shaming, and Tracking Device [Blog]. *Schools Matter.* http://www.schoolsmatter.info/2014/11/classdojo-another-insecure-chilld.html

[82] Rose, N. (1996). *Inventing our Selves: Psychology, Power, and Personhood.* Cambridge University Press. https://doi.org/10.1017/CBO9780511752179

[83] Popkewitz, T. S. (2012). Numbers in grids of intelligibility: Making sense of how educational truth is told. In *Educating for the Knowledge Economy?* Routledge.

[84] *New Vision for Education: Fostering Social and Emotional Learning Through Technology.* (2016, March 10). World Economic Forum. https://www.weforum.org/publications/new-vision-for-education-fostering-social-and-emotional-learning-through-technology/

[85] Manolev, J., Sullivan, A., & Slee, R. (2019). The datafication of discipline: ClassDojo, surveillance and a performative classroom

culture. *Learning, Media and Technology, 44*(1), 36–51.
https://doi.org/10.1080/17439884.2018.1558237

[86] Elias, A. A. (2012, October 6). Hadith on Fitrah: Every child born to
believe in Allah. *Daily Hadith Online.*
https://www.abuaminaelias.com/dailyhadithonline/2012/10/06/
every-child-born-fitrah-nature/

[87] Barna, G. (2023). *Raising Spiritual Champions: Nurturing Your Child's
Heart, Mind and Soul.* Arizona Christian University Press.
https://georgebarna.com/product/raising-spiritual-champions-
book/

[88] Thompson, D. F. (2007). *What is Practical Ethics?* Edmond and Lily
Safra Center for Ethics, Harvard University.
https://www.ethics.harvard.edu/what-practical-ethics

[89] Elias, A. A. (2023, May 14). Hadith on Akhlaq: Faith is completed by
excellent character [Blog]. *Daily Hadith Online - The Teachings of
Prophet Muhammad (Saw).*
https://www.abuaminaelias.com/dailyhadithonline/2023/05/14/
faith-completed/

[90] Elias, A. A. (2023a, May 13). Hadith on Akhlaq: Good character
nearest to the Prophet. *Daily Hadith Online - The Teachings of Prophet
Muhammad (Saw).*
https://www.abuaminaelias.com/dailyhadithonline/2023/05/14/
good-character-nearest/

[91] Deccani, A. H. (2016, May 6). Rabi Ibn Amer رضي الله تعالىٰ عنه explains
the mission of Islam to the Persian King, Rustum: *THE
ISLAMIC WAY OF LIFE.*
https://theislamicreality.blogspot.com/2016/05/rabi-ibn-amer-
explains-mission-of-islam.html

[92] Lampert, L. L. (2020). *ClassDojo and Home-School Communication*
[Ed.D., New Jersey City University].
https://www.proquest.com/docview/2627082551/abstract/E804
696B4BE34A46PQ/1

[93] Elias, A. A. (2023b, May 13). Hadith on Akhlaq: The best of you,
the worst of you [Blog]. Daily Hadith Online - *The Teachings of*

Prophet Muhammad (Saw).
https://www.abuaminaelias.com/dailyhadithonline/2023/05/14/best-and-worst/

[94] Lamb, J. (2024, September 6). *Principal Lamb's Daily Memo Template.* ClassDojo.

[95] Elias, A. A. (2014a, May 9). Hadith on Zina: Would you like that for your mother, sister? [Blog]. Daily Hadith Online - *The Teachings of Prophet Muhammad (Saw).*
https://www.abuaminaelias.com/dailyhadithonline/2014/05/09/zina-adulter-like-sister/

[96] *Al-Adab Al-Mufrad 239—Cheerfulness Towards People—* كِتَاب الإنْبِسَاطِ إِلَى النَّاس—*Sunnah.com—Sayings and Teachings of Prophet Muhammad (* صلى الله عليه و سلم*).* (n.d.). Sunnah.Com. Retrieved December 10, 2024, from https://sunnah.com/adab:239

[97] *Hadith 19, 40 Hadith an-Nawawi—Forty Hadith of an-Nawawi—Sayings and Teachings of Prophet Muhammad (*صلى الله عليه و سلم*).* (n.d.). Sunnah.Com. Retrieved September 4, 2024, from https://sunnah.com/nawawi40:19

[98] King, J. E. (1991). Dysconscious Racism: Ideology, Identity, and the Miseducation of Teachers. *The Journal of Negro Education, 60*(2), 133–146. https://doi.org/10.2307/2295605

[99] Miller, E. (2021). *Determinants of Change and Technology Adoption in K-12 Schools* [M.S.Ed., University of Victoria]. http://hdl.handle.net/1828/12958

[100] International Society for Technology in Education. (n.d.-a). *ISTE Standards.* ISTE. Retrieved September 24, 2024, from https://iste.org/standards

www.ingramcontent.com/pod-product-compliance
Lightning Source LLC
LaVergne TN
LVHW051631080426
835511LV00016B/2297